Understand Music Theory

To Lurch, who slept through it all

Understand Music Theory

Margaret Richer

For UK order enquiries: please contact Bookpoint Ltd, 130 Milton Park, Abingdon, Oxon OX14 4SB. Telephone: +44 (0) 1235 827720. Fax: +44 (0) 1235 400454. Lines are open 09.00–17.00, Monday to Saturday, with a 24-hour message answering service. Details about our titles and how to order are available at www.teachyourself.com

For USA order enquiries: please contact McGraw-Hill Customer Services, PO Box 545, Blacklick, OH 43004-0545, USA. Telephone: 1-800-722-4726. Fax: 1-614-755-5645.

For Canada order enquiries: please contact McGraw-Hill Ryerson Ltd, 300 Water St, Whitby, Ontario L1N 9B6, Canada. Telephone: 905 430 5000. Fax: 905 430 5020.

Long renowned as the authoritative source for self-guided learning – with more than 50 million copies sold worldwide – the **Teach Yourself** series includes over 500 titles in the fields of languages, crafts, hobbies, business, computing and education.

British Library Cataloguing in Publication Data: a catalogue record for this title is available from the British Library.

Library of Congress Catalog Card Number: on file.

First published in UK 2002 by Hodder Education, part of Hachette UK, 338 Euston Road, London NW1 3BH.

First published in US 2002 by The McGraw-Hill Companies, Inc.

This edition published 2010.

Previously published as *Teach Yourself Music Theory*.

The **Teach Yourself** name is a registered trade mark of Hodder Headline.

Copyright © 2002, 2003, 2010 Margaret Richer

Typeset by MPS Limited, A Macmillan Company.

Printed in Great Britain for Hodder Education, an Hachette UK Company, 338 Euston Road, London NW1 3BH, by CPI Cox & Wyman, Reading, Berkshire RG1 8EX.

The publisher has used its best endeavours to ensure that the URLs for external websites referred to in this book are correct and active at the time of going to press. However, the publisher and the author have no responsibility for the websites and can make no guarantee that a site will remain live or that the content will remain relevant, decent or appropriate.

Hachette UK's policy is to use papers that are natural, renewable and recyclable products and made from wood grown in sustainable forests. The logging and manufacturing processes are expected to conform to the environmental regulations of the country of origin.

Impression number   10 9 8 7 6 5 4 3 2

Year   2014 2013 2012

Acknowledgements

I would like to thank Helen Hart, Sue Hart, Catherine Coe and other staff at Hodder & Stoughton for their help at various stages in producing this book. Thanks also go to friends and neighbours who listened attentively to my ideas and gave encouragement. Finally, I thank all the people I have taught throughout the years. Without them, this book would not have been possible.

A note on terms

British English has been used as the primary language, but US equivalents have been given where necessary.

Contents

Meet the author

Welcome to *Understand Music Theory*, a practical approach to learning the mechanics of music. I have written this book so that it is suitable for absolute beginners as well as those with some musical knowledge. Other than a CD player, no special materials are needed. A music manuscript notebook with printed staff lines would be useful for completing some of the written exercises, although space has been provided in the book itself.

Because I know that it is difficult to learn music theory without applying it, *Understand Music Theory* takes the fundamentals and presents them with easy-to-follow explanations, examples and exercises. By following the practical approach that I have devised, I hope you will gain knowledge through active learning, giving you a clearer understanding which is based on doing rather than just memorizing facts. The book begins with summaries which enable the reader to dip in and sample the book. I have written one-minute, five-minute and ten-minute sections summarizing key points and providing a core base of knowledge before tackling the whole book.

Learning music theory takes time, practice and repetition. I have broken each new concept into small chapters followed by exercises, which reinforce the material by a variety of written, listening and practical work. Any activity involving the use of the CD is clearly marked by the sign ⊚. Clear instructions are also given on the CD before an activity begins. Goals to confirm understanding are included at the end of each chapter, as are any answers to the exercises. Although the exercises themselves do not provide adequate training, I am sure that they will help in exploring the facts and provide an introduction to aural and listening skills. The book is arranged so that each chapter builds on what has already been presented, so should be followed in strict order. Throughout the book I have noted my own 'insights' to add a personal touch, and the final 'Test yourself' section at the end of each chapter assesses the learner's readiness to move on.

In writing *Understand Music Theory* I have made sure that it contains information that can be applied to all types of music, whether instrumental or vocal, classical or popular. Useful charts, tables and a glossary are found at the back of the book for quick reference. I have also given a few suggestions for further study, including use of the internet. I hope you find the book useful and also enjoy the new musical knowledge that you will acquire.

Only got a minute?

You may be asking yourself, 'What actually is music theory?', 'What will I need to learn?' Briefly, music theory is all about exploring the fascinating mechanics of music. Like any subject, it contains certain elements. In music, the terms used for these elements are rhythm, pitch, melody and harmony. To understand the theory of music, you will not only need to know and understand the terms used, but also develop practical skills. This summary will give you an overview of what is involved.

Rhythm is broadly defined as anything associated with the length of a sound. Notes of varying shapes, held for different lengths, are joined together in patterns to form rhythm. It is first necessary to understand and learn the various note values. You must also learn to count evenly when performing rhythms.

Pitch is used to indicate the highness or lowness of a musical sound. Musical pitches are given letter-names based on the first seven letters of the alphabet, and written on a musical staff. Learning to read pitches takes patience and time, but is necessary if you want to progress further.

A **melody** is an organized series of different pitches. The notes are given time values and arranged in a time signature. The knowledge of intervals (the distances between pitches), both writing and hearing, plus the understanding of the construction of scales and their key signatures are needed for working with melody.

The study of chords, a chord being three or more pitches played or sung together, is **harmony**. You will need to learn about the different types of chords, their construction and functions.

There are many other musical terms, some used for expression, such as tempo (speed) and dynamics (volume). Also, form or overall organization of different types of music needs to be learned. This is just the beginning. I hope you will want to read on!

5 Only got five minutes?

Music theory is the science of music. It is all about exploring its mechanics, but why study it? As with any subject, certain basic elements are needed. It is necessary to understand the terms used and know what the various signs and symbols mean in order to participate at any level, whether as a listener or performer. Let's start by discussing the different elements.

The first element, **rhythm**, is broadly defined as anything associated with the duration or length of sound. It is represented by notes of various shapes which are held for different lengths of time. They are joined together in patterns to form rhythms. Notation of rhythms includes many signs and symbols besides the notes. A time signature is found at the beginning of a piece.

When making music, it is important to understand the notation of the different note values and to be able to count accurately in various time signatures. If the rhythm is wrong, your tune will not be recognized. Also, when working in a group, other performers will not slow down or stop just because you do!

Now let's have a look at the element of **pitch**, the lowness or highness of a sound. Musical pitches are given letter-names based on the first seven letters of the alphabet, and are written as notes on a staff of five lines and four spaces.

Besides the musical notes themselves, there are other important signs related to pitches. Sharps, flats and accidentals are used to raise and lower pitch.

Leaving pitch for the moment, let's talk about **melody**, another important element found in music. A melody consists of an organized series of different pitches. They are given time values and arranged in a time signature. A good melody has a sense of direction called its melodic curve, and uses such devices as repetition and small melodic patterns to hold it together.

The last element, **harmony**, involves the study of chords. Three or more notes sounded together make a chord, but there is no limit to the number of notes. The simplest type of chord is the triad, consisting of three pitches. The two basic types of triad are major and minor.

So far, we have looked at the four basic elements of rhythm, pitch, melody and harmony. These elements need to be organized by a basic plan called **form**. There are different ways to hold a work together, repetition being one of the most commonly used. Musical form is also represented by using letters that label repeated material and new sections.

Before ending this summary, I would like to mention a few other important aspects of music theory. Although an individual performance depends on the arrangement, interpretation and personal taste, the composer does give some indications by using certain signs and words to show desired tempo (speed), dynamics (volume) and overall feeling. Many of the terms are in Italian, the international language of music.

This summary would not be complete without a mention of music theory in the 20th century and beyond. The theory has used a wide range of ideas from the past and combined them in new ways. Contemporary music often sounds odd to listeners because of the new methods used in its composition. The best way to approach this music is to listen with an open mind, and not compare it with music written in a more traditional way. Indications for the future show that there will not only be further experimentation, but also interesting new uses of established practices.

10 Only got ten minutes?

When listening to music, have you ever wondered what it consists of, or why it sounds as it does? In this summary, I will try to answer these questions by exploring the numerous elements that are combined to make a piece of music, plus the knowledge and skills needed to understand and perform music.

Each element is not contained in every work. It is difficult to discuss each individually because they are all dependent on each other. However, **rhythm** does have more of an identity of its own. It can be free, with no regular pulse to help organize it. Most music, however, does have a regular pulse, similar to an underlying heartbeat. Music is written down as notes that are combined into patterns to form rhythm.

The shape of a note shows how long it is held. It is important to learn to recognize the shapes of notes and to write them correctly, as each one represents a different value. Bar-lines are vertical lines that divide written music into equal blocks. When actually performing, it is important to remember to give the first beat in each bar a slight accent, although it is not notated in the music. The time signature is written at the start of a piece. It contains two numbers resembling a fraction. The top number shows the number of beats in each bar while the bottom one identifies the type of note getting the basic beat.

Let's leave the basics of rhythm now and explore another element found in music, the **melody**. Briefly defined, a melody is an organized series of pitches combined with rhythm. A **pitch** is the lowness or highness of a sound. Musical pitches are given letter-names based on the first seven letters of the alphabet and are written as notes on a staff of five lines and four spaces. As an aid to learning about high and low pitch, the use of a piano keyboard is useful. Learning to read pitches is difficult and requires repetition and reinforcement.

An interval is the space between two pitches. It is necessary to have a thorough understanding and working knowledge of intervals, as scales and chords are based on their arrangement.

Scales are the alphabetical successions of notes beginning on a particular pitch. The pitches of any scale are called degrees. All music is composed using some form of scale. Scales sound different from one another because of the arrangements of the pitches. For approximately the past 400 years, most music in the Western world has used major or minor scales.

A major scale is a series of semitones and whole tones arranged in a specific order, and this arrangement identifies it as major in sound. The notes of a C major scale are found by playing just the white keys of a piano from any C to the C one octave (eight keys) higher. Music using these pitches with C as the starting note or keynote is said to be in the key of C major.

The minor scale follows a different pattern of pitches, and unlike the major, is found in three forms. These are called the natural, harmonic and melodic. The forms of minor scale used may vary within a piece, with both the harmonic and melodic appearing. Because of this, music is said to be in a minor key, not harmonic or melodic.

A key signature is the information found at the beginning of a work showing the sharps and flats required. There are different sets of key signatures for major and minor scales. Proper notation of the sharps or flats is very important in identifying the keys.

This brings us to a new subject, **harmony**, the study of chords. Whereas two notes sounded together are considered to be an interval, three or more notes form a chord. There is no limit to the number of notes in a chord. The notes of a chord can also be spread throughout the various instruments of an entire symphony orchestra. The simplest type of chord is the triad, consisting of three notes.

Adding chord accompaniment to a given melody is a very important skill in the study of harmony. The complete study of adding chords and chord progressions is lengthy, but there are a few basic steps involved in adding a simple chord accompaniment to a melody. It is helpful to make a chord chart showing the names of the notes found in each triad. By using the chart, you are able to see which chords would be the most logical to use. Of course, listening helps in deciding which chords are the most logical. It is also necessary to learn to transpose both melody and accompaniment. Many times music is written in a key that is difficult to sing or play, so it needs to be moved to a more suitable key. However, if everything isn't transposed correctly, the whole thing will sound wrong!

Now that we have talked about rhythm, melody and harmony, a few basic points about **musical form** are in order. The elements of music need to be organized by a basic plan or roadmap called form. Form is often represented by letters, with each repetition of the same material having the same letter. A strophic piece has the same music repeated in each verse, so its form would be A A A A. Church hymns and folk songs often use this form. Music consisting of two alternating melodies would be diagrammed as A B A B, which is called binary form. Musical form ranges from a simple strophic piece to the composite form of the orchestral symphony, which contains several large sections called movements.

Have you ever wondered why the same piece of music played by different performers sounds unique? Much of this is due to the arrangement, interpretation and personal taste of the conductor and the artists. The composer does give some indications by using certain signs and words to show the desired speed (tempo), dynamics (volume) and overall feeling of the work.

In a general way, expression means anything about the quality of a performance, including such things as phrasing, speed and volume. It is everything that gives individuality to a performance. Dynamics deal exclusively with degrees of volume of sound. Words or signs are written above the staff at the beginning of a piece, with new instructions given throughout. They are generally indicated by Italian terms and individual letters. It is important that the music notation shows where the gradual dynamic changes both start and end.

Instructions for phrasing and articulation are also used to help in the interpretation of music. A phrase is similar to a phrase or clause in a line of writing, and is several bars long. Phrases are notated by a long, curved line starting from the first note and ending at the last note of the phrase. Articulation refers to the way an individual note or group of notes should be performed.

This brings me to the final topic of the summary, a discussion of music theory in contemporary music. Some of the music from the 20th century and beyond is written in a completely different way from earlier compositions. First of all, rhythms have become more free and irregular. Besides this, the traditional structure of triads has changed. Even some of the traditional musical instruments have been used differently. There is no doubt that the possibilities of new music are endless!

1

Introducing rhythm

To create any work of art, certain basic elements are needed.
In music, these include rhythm, pitch, melody, harmony and tone
colour, although each element is not contained in every piece of
music. It is difficult to discuss each element individually because
they are all dependent on one another when composing music.
Rhythm, however, does have more of an identity of its own.
In this chapter, you will be introduced to the basics of reading,
writing and performing rhythm.

In musical terms, rhythm may be broadly defined as anything
associated with the duration or length of a sound. It can be
completely free, having no basic pulse or divisions to help organize
it. Free use of rhythm is found in some primitive music, oriental
music and sometimes modern jazz. Most music, however, has a
regular pulse, rather like an underlying heartbeat. Musical sounds
are written as notes held for different lengths. These notes are
combined into patterns forming rhythm.

Note values

This is an example of a music note:

It is the symbol used to show musical sound.   ♩ ← Stem
                                                  ← Head

Written music indicates how long a note should sound by its shape. The grouping together of notes of varying lengths creates rhythm. The following table shows the shapes of three notes you will learn in this chapter. The British terms, followed by the American, are given. It is helpful to refer to the notes as whole, half and quarter because this shows how their values relate to each other.

Semibreve (whole note)	𝅝
Minim (half note – lasts half the length of a whole note)	𝅗𝅥
Crotchet (quarter note – lasts a quarter of a whole note)	𝅘𝅥
Here's how the note values relate to one another.	𝅝

Vertical lines which divide written music into equal segments are called bar-lines. The space between two bar-lines is called a bar or measure. Two vertical lines, a thin followed by a thick one, show the end of a work. Two thin vertical lines indicate the end of a major section of a large work.

When performing, count evenly as though the bar-lines do not exist. There is a very slight accent on the first beat of each bar although this is not shown by notation. Music notes are placed on a staff having five lines and four spaces. The position of the note on the staff shows its pitch: whether it sounds high or low. Because this chapter deals only with rhythm, the staff lines will not be used at this point.

Bars and bar-lines

bar-line

| Bar
(measure) | | | ‖ End

Time signatures

At the beginning of a piece of music, you will find two numbers
resembling a fraction. (Note, however, that there is *no* line dividing
the two numbers.) This is called the time signature or metre. The
top number tells how many beats are in each bar. The bottom
number tells the type of note which gets the basic beat. The most
common time signature used is $\frac{4}{4}$ time. The top 4 indicates four
beats in every bar. The bottom 4 shows that the crotchet (quarter
note) gets one beat. Occasionally, a C sign is used for the time
signature instead of the numbers. I find it helpful to think of
a pie. One whole pie contains two halves and four quarters:

4 = how many beats in each bar

4 = type of note; crotchet (quarter note) gets one beat

Insight

When learning to recognize note values, it is not only helpful
to draw and divide pies, you can also turn pies back into
notes! This is done by adding a stem to a pie containing two
halves. It will then look like a minim. Filling in a pie made of
four quarters and giving it a stem will turn it into a crotchet.
It is important to learn to recognize these basic shapes!

Remember, the time signature shows the number of *beats*, not
the number of *notes*, per bar. Notes of various lengths are mixed
together in a bar of music. They must add up to the proper number
of beats required by the time signature.

Exercise 1.1 (Listening)

First look through the examples that follow. On the CD, you will
hear each example demonstrated, once with counting, then
once without. There are two introductory bars counted before
each example to set the pace. Now listen to the CD and see
if you are able to follow the notation.

(Contd)

These practice tips listed will be helpful in learning to play rhythms correctly.

1 *Always look through the music first, noting anything particularly difficult.*
2 *Count one or two bars before you start, to establish the speed.*
3 *Set the speed slow enough so you will be able to keep a steady pace.*
4 *When you are clapping a rhythm, keep your hands together to indicate you are holding a note of a longer value.*
5 *If you have problems keeping an even pace, try using a metronome. These are available as a wind-up instrument which ticks or as an electric model with a flashing light. The beats on an electric keyboard may also be used.*
6 *Instead of clapping, exercises may also be practised at a keyboard. Using one finger, select one key and play the rhythm. Remember to hold notes for their full value.*
7 *Singers might pick a sound such as 'la' and sing the rhythm on one pitch.*

Insight

Always remember to perform rhythms at a steady pace. When practising alone, it is tempting to forget about the pulse. When you begin to play music with others, it will soon be evident that they are not going to slow down or stop just because you do ... nor will your electronic keyboard accompaniment follow your fluctuations!

Exercise 1.2 (Practical)

Here are some rhythms for you to clap. Before turning on the CD, look through the exercises to make sure you have a general understanding of the material. Each exercise has two bars of count before you begin clapping. The correct rhythm will be demonstrated immediately after your performance.

a) $\frac{4}{4}$ 1 2 3 4 | 1 2 3 4 | ♩ ♩ ♩ ♩ | ♩ ♩ ♩ | ♩ ♩ ♩ | 𝅝 ‖

b) $\frac{4}{4}$ 1 2 3 4 | 1 2 3 4 | ♩ ♩ ♩ | ♩ ♩ ♩ ♩ | ♩ ♩ ♩ ♩ | ♩ ♩ ♩ ‖

c) $\frac{4}{4}$ 1 2 3 4 | 1 2 3 4 | ♩ ♩ ♩ | ♩ ♩ ♩ | ♩ | ♩ ♩ ♩ | ♩ ♩ ♩ ‖

Notation

A stem may either go up or down from the note head. If the stem goes up, it is placed on the right. If the stem goes down, it is placed on the left. More will be mentioned about notation of stems in later chapters.

Examples of stems ♩ ♪

Spacing of the notes in the bar is important. The following examples show how proper spacing helps in reading music notation. Study the first bar of example a). The minim (half note) takes up twice as much space as the two crotchets (quarter notes). The relationship is expressed visually.

a) $\frac{4}{4}$ ♩ ♩ ♩ | ♩ ♩ | ♩ ♩ ♩ | 𝅝 ‖

Example b) is an example of poor spacing. There are the correct number of beats in each bar, but the notes are incorrectly spaced. The first and second crotchets (quarter notes) are placed so that it appears they take up most of the first bar when actually they only occupy the first two beats. The two minims in the second bar should be evenly spaced. In the last bar, the semibreve should be placed at the beginning of the bar because it is played on the first beat and held through the rest of the bar.

b) $\frac{4}{4}$ ♩ ♩ ♩ | ♩ ♩ | ♩ ♩ ♩ | 𝅝 ‖

Insight

In my experience, many students find rhythm difficult to understand. If a poorly notated musical rhythm is used, the problem is only made worse. A rhythm written out properly, showing the relationships between the note values, really helps in learning about rhythm.

Exercise 1.3 (Written)

The following are examples of rhythms written in the time signature of $\frac{4}{4}$. Each is four bars long but each bar is incorrect in some way. Correct each exercise in the space below it. You may need to add stems, fill in the heads of the notes or add some notes. There may be more than one correct solution to each. The spacing gives some clues. I've completed the first one for you. The answers are at the end of this chapter.

For further practice, try clapping your completed written work. Remember to follow the practice tips.

Exercise 1.4 (Practical)

It is important to be able to hear a rhythm and write it down.
The following exercises will help you develop the skill by using
rhythm dictation. A 'skeleton' of six bars follows. The first two are
for establishing the beat and should be left blank. The following
four bars are for writing down the rhythm you hear on the CD.
The rhythm will be repeated five times. On each repeat, you
should be able to add notes until you have written down the
entire four bars.

$\frac{4}{4}$ 1 2 3 4 | 1 2 3 4 | | | | ‖

Time signature of $\frac{2}{4}$

In the time signature of $\frac{2}{4}$ there are two beats in each bar. The
crotchet (quarter note) still gets one beat. There is an accent on the
first beat of each bar, followed by a weaker second beat. Think of
marching: left right, left right, left right … the left foot is heavier!
Study the example, which shows four bars written in $\frac{2}{4}$ time.

$\frac{2}{4}$ ♩ ♩ | ♩ ♩ | ♩ ♩ | ♩ ‖

strong weak

....
Insight
It is easy to learn to feel the difference between 2 and 4 time.
First, practise your marching in 2. In 4, the heavy foot only
happens half as often. The 'strong' is on the first beat only,
followed by three 'weaks'. Compare the two.
....

Correct the following exercises by adding notes or stems or filling in the heads of the notes.

a) $\frac{2}{4}$ ♩ ♩ | ♩ ♩ | ♩ ♩ | 𝅝 ‖

Correct Version $\frac{2}{4}$

b) $\frac{2}{4}$ ♩ 𝅝 | ♩ ♩ | 𝅝 | ♩ ♩ ‖

Correct Version $\frac{2}{4}$

c) $\frac{2}{4}$ ♩ | 𝅝 | ♩ 𝅝 | ♩ ‖

Correct Version $\frac{2}{4}$

Exercise 1.6 (Practical)

Here are some rhythms for you to clap. There are two bars of count before you begin. The correct rhythm is performed immediately after your clapping.

a) $\frac{2}{4}$ 1 2 | 1 2 | ♩ ♩ | ♩ | ♩ | ♩ ♩ | ♩ | ♩ | ♩ ♩ | ♩ ‖

b) $\frac{2}{4}$ 1 2 | 1 2 | ♩ ♩ | ♩ ♩ | ♩ | ♩ ♩ | ♩ ♩ | ♩ | ♩ ♩ | ♩ ‖

Rests

There is a corresponding symbol for each note value that means you do not play a sound. There is silence – you are resting! The symbol is called a rest and is used instead of the note.

𝄽 = ♩   𝄼 = ♩   𝄼 = 𝅝

(sits on a line when written on the staff)

(hangs down from a line when written on the staff)

Here is an example using rests. If an entire bar is silent, use the semibreve rest no matter what time signature is used.

$$\begin{array}{c} 4 \\ 4 \end{array} \quad \textrm{♩ ♩ ♩ ₹} \mid \textrm{♩} - \mid - \mid \textrm{♩ ₹ ♩ ₹} \parallel$$

Try drawing a few crotchet (quarter note) rests. You will produce a reasonable rest by first drawing an 'M' on its side, then adding a 'c' to the bottom.

When clapping rhythms, keep your hands together to indicate holding a note, but take your hands apart when counting a rest. On the keyboard, lift your finger to observe the rest. If singing, don't hold the sound through the rest. Observing silence is important. It adds interest to music. Clap the next two examples. The first one is quite boring. The second is much more interesting. What a difference six rests can make!

a) $\begin{array}{c} 4 \\ 4 \end{array}$ ♩ ♩ ♩ ♩ | ♩ ♩ ♩ ♩ | ♩ ♩ ♩ ♩ | ♩ ♩ ♩ ♩ ‖

b) $\begin{array}{c} 4 \\ 4 \end{array}$ ♩ ₹ ♩ ♩ | ₹ ♩ ♩ ₹ | ♩ ₹ ♩ ♩ | ₹ ♩ ♩ ₹ ‖

Exercise 1.7 (Written)

Complete the exercises by adding one rest where the 'R' appears.

a) $\begin{array}{c} 4 \\ 4 \end{array}$ ♩   ♩ R | R ♩ ♩ ♩ | R | R   ♩ ‖

b) $\begin{array}{c} 2 \\ 4 \end{array}$ ♩   R | R | ♩   R | R   ♩ ‖

Insight

In clapping exercises, it may seem silly to be so concerned about holding your hands apart when counting a rest. However, it is good training for when you are performing more advanced music, and could save you embarrassment. You don't want to be holding a note when all of the other performers are silent!

Tempo

Tempo is the speed at which music is played. Rhythm refers to the way notes of different lengths are grouped into patterns. A rhythm may be played quickly or slowly. The rhythm itself never changes, but the speed can. In the four bars that follow, the rhythm stays the same whether it is performed slowly or quickly. Try clapping it at different speeds.

Tempo markings are found at the beginning of a piece of music. Sometimes the marking is in English. Italian, however, is the international musical language, so many terms are given in Italian.

Here are a few terms relating to tempo. There is a list of Italian terms in the glossary at the end of the book:

allegro = quick
largo = slow
presto = very fast
andante = walking pace

 Exercise 1.8 (Practical)

The following rhythms are written in two parts. They may be performed by two people or two groups. The note stems go upwards in the top part while the lower part has stems going downwards. This is done purely to help separate the two parts. Notice how important the spacing is when writing for more than one part. The notes need to line up vertically. Two-part exercises are also suitable for individual practice. One hand should tap the top part while the other hand taps the bottom.

On the CD, two bars of introductory count are given. For the first exercise, the bottom line is recorded and the student should clap the top. For the second exercise, the top line is recorded and the student claps the bottom. This gives you practice playing with someone else.

When playing with others, you must keep going, even if you make a mistake. No one else is going to stop and wait for you!

Exercise 1.9 (Practical)

This final exercise provides listening practice in the form of leader/follower. On the CD you will hear a short rhythm followed by a silence. Listen closely to the rhythm given by the 'leader' and then clap it immediately in the following silence. The rhythms vary in length. Don't worry if you can't do them all. Try to keep going. There is not time to stop and correct yourself. There will be two bars of count at the beginning before the 'leader' starts.

GOALS

Before moving on, make sure you know the following:

1 *The names and note values of* o d d.
2 *What the top and bottom numbers of the time signatures indicate.*
3 *The function of rests.*
4 *Practice tips for performing rhythms.*
5 *The importance of correct musical notation, including spacing between notes.*
6 *The difference between tempo and rhythm.*

Answers

EXERCISE 1.3

b) 𝄴 ♩ ♩ ♩ | ♩ ♩ ♩ ♩ | ♩ ♩ ♩ | ♩ ♩ 𝄂

c) 𝄴 ♩ ♩ ♩ ♩ | ♩ ♩ ♩ | ♩ ♩ | ♩ ♩ ♩ 𝄂

EXERCISE 1.4

𝄴 1 2 3 4 | 1 2 3 4 | ♩ ♩ ♩ ♩ | ♩ ♩ | ♩ ♩ ♩ | 𝅝 𝄂

EXERCISE 1.5

a) 𝄔 ♩ ♩ | ♩ ♩ | ♩ ♩ | ♩ 𝄂

b) 𝄔 ♩ ♩ | ♩ ♩ | ♩ | ♩ ♩ 𝄂

c) 𝄔 ♩ ♩ | ♩ | ♩ ♩ | ♩ ♩ 𝄂

   or
   ♩ ♩

EXERCISE 1.7

a) 𝄴 ♩ ♩ 𝄽 | 𝄽 ♩ ♩ ♩ | – | – ♩ 𝄂

b) 𝄔 ♩ 𝄽 | – | ♩ 𝄽 | 𝄽 ♩ 𝄂

TEST YOURSELF

1 *Give a brief definition of rhythm.*

2 *How are musical sounds written?*

3 *What indicates how long a note should sound?*

4 *Describe a bar-line.*

5 *What do the top and bottom numbers of a time signature tell?*

6 *Give another name for a crotchet.*

7 *Why is it important to use proper spacing when notating music?*

8 *How many beats to a bar with the top number of 2?*

9 *Name the symbol used to indicate silence.*

10 *Define tempo.*

2

Pitch

In this chapter, we will leave rhythm for the moment and start exploring the element of pitch. In music theory, the word 'pitch' is used to indicate the lowness or highness of a sound. Technically, pitch is determined by the number of vibrations per second or frequency of a sound. The faster the vibration, the higher the pitch. Low sounds, therefore, have a slow frequency. Musical pitches are given letter-names based on the first seven letters of the alphabet and are written as notes on a staff. Before going any further, let's stop and concentrate on learning more about high and low pitch by using the keyboard as a means of demonstration.

The keyboard and musical alphabet

There are seven letters used in music, called the musical alphabet. They are A, B, C, D, E, F and G. The keyboard diagram (Figure 2.1) shows how the seven letter-names are arranged and repeated up and down the keys of the keyboard. Moving upwards (to the right)

the sounds become higher in pitch, and moving downwards (to the left) the sounds become lower in pitch.

Exercise 2.1 (Practical)

On the CD, you will first hear a demonstration of pitches moving upwards (higher) from middle C, then moving lower. You will then hear a second series of pitches for you to identity as high or low. Listen carefully to each sound as it is played. Write down whether you think it is higher in pitch or lower than the previous sound. An example will be given on the CD before you start the exercise.

EXERCISE

Insight

If you have use of a piano or electronic keyboard, it would be helpful for you to actually play a series of keys, first moving up, then down. The pitches you play are not important, but you will gain more practice listening for the difference between high and low sounds.

GROUPINGS OF KEYS

It is important to understand fully the arrangement of the keyboard, as this will be an aid in learning about the different aspects of music theory presented in this book. Take a few minutes to study the picture of the keyboard. You will find there are both white and black keys. The black keys are arranged in groups of two and three. I like to refer to these groups as 'landmarks'. They are helpful in locating the white keys and generally finding your way around the keyboard. Always try to be aware of how the keys relate to one another. Notice, for example, how D is located in the middle of the two black keys. One key up (higher) from D is E. When moving upwards, say the musical alphabet forwards. One key down (lower) from D is C. When moving downwards, the alphabet runs backwards.

Exercise 2.2 (Practical)

Using the keyboard diagram, practise locating the following:
a) All the groups of two black keys, up and down the keyboard.
b) Point to all the Ds, then all the Es.
c) Locate all the groups of three black keys.
d) Find all the Fs. (This is the white key located just to the left of the three black keys.)
e) Find all the Gs, As and Bs.

 Exercise 2.3 (Practical)

This exercise is designed to help you develop speed in finding your way around the keyboard. You will be asked to locate various keys on your diagram. There will be a space between each instruction to give you ample time to find what you are looking for.

Insight

Besides listening to the CD, actually playing the keys asked for in Exercise 2.2 will help in learning your way around the keyboard. If you have access to a 'real live' keyboard, you will be able to hear the sounds of the keys you have been asked to locate on the diagram.

The staff

Music notes are written on a staff consisting of five lines and the four spaces between the lines. The plural of 'staff' is 'staves'. The placement of the note shows its pitch: whether its sound is high or low. A note may be written on a line, as if the line is running through it. This is then called a 'line' note. Notes may also be placed in the spaces between the lines. These are 'space' notes. Be sure to remember that 'notes' are written on the staff. 'Keys' are found on the keyboard. You do not play the 'notes' of a keyboard … you play the 'keys'.

Examples of line notes   Examples of space notes

A clef sign is found at the beginning of each staff. The treble clef,
also called the G clef, curls around the second line. A note with
the second line running through it is the pitch of G. This is a good
landmark when reading music. Try drawing a few treble clefs.
It is easiest to start with the vertical line followed by the top curve.
The final curl should be around the second line.

MIDDLE C

There is a theory that the musical staff did not always consist of just
five lines and four spaces. As early music evolved, more lines were
added until there were 11. This became difficult to read, so the line
in the middle was removed. It now appears as a short line called a
leger or ledger line. This line is used for the note of middle C. Piano
music is written using two staves joined together by a brace. This
is called the grand staff. In general, the notes for the right hand are
written on the upper staff, using the treble clef. The notes for the
left hand are written on the lower staff, using the bass clef.

Staff with 11 lines

Middle C may be written in two ways. When it is to be played by
the right hand, it appears nearer the upper staff as shown in the

following example. If middle C is to be played by the left hand, it appears nearer the bass clef.

Grand staff showing positions of middle C

Beginning to read notes in treble and bass clef

NOTES IN THE TREBLE CLEF

You will now start learning to recognize the different pitches as they are written as notes on the staff. Only a few notes will be introduced at one time to make learning easier. Here are the first five notes of the treble clef, starting with middle C. The lowest line, E, is called the first line and the first space is F. Notice that the space beneath the staff (created by the leger line middle C and the first line E) is used to place the note D.

Five notes in treble clef

C D E F G

When reading music, the relationship in movement between the notes is important. Notice whether a note moves up or down and by step or skip. A step is when movement is to a note directly above or below the previous one. An example is E followed by F, a line note moving to a space note. If a line note moves to another line note, there has obviously been a skip. Skips may be small (C moving up to E) or larger (C moving up to G).

Insight

Understanding movement by steps and skips is an essential part of reading music. To gain practice, study any piece of music notation. Identify the movement between pitches. Do this often, using a variety of music. It all helps!

Exercise 2.4 (Written)

Here is a series of notes for you to identify by name. Write the letter-names of the notes under each using semibreves (whole notes). Don't worry about adding stems or filling in the note heads. This exercise is purely for practice in reading pitches and does not involve rhythms.

Now write your own series, then go back and write the names under each one.

NOTES IN THE BASS CLEF

Study the five notes written here in bass clef.

Five notes in bass clef

The bass clef is also called the F clef. Two dots are placed on each side of the fourth line, F. You will probably find it more difficult to remember these new notes because they do not move in a straightforward alphabetical order. Establishing landmarks will help you in your music reading. Middle C is a good landmark as it is easy to recognize. Remembering that the two dots surround the F line is also helpful.

Insight

Remember that reading music does not only involve recognizing individual pitch names. All of the notes move in relation to each other. By using landmarks, it is a lot easier to figure out the more difficult notes. Besides the landmarks I have suggested, find some others that work for you.

EXERCISE

Exercise 2.5 (Written)

Write the names underneath each of the semibreves (whole notes).

— — — — — — — — —

Write your own series, then go back and add the name under each.

— — — — — — —

Exercise 2.6 (Practical)

Remembering the names of the notes takes time and repetition. This exercise provides further practice in learning the notes of the staff. On the CD, you will hear the names of notes given. Write each one down on the following staff, making sure you use the correct clef. The answers are given at the end of the chapter.

GOALS

1 Define 'pitch'.
2 Know the letters used in the musical alphabet.
3 Know the arrangement of the keys on the keyboard and be able to locate them quickly.
4 Read and write the notes of middle C, D, E, F, G in treble clef.
5 Read and write the notes of F, G, A, B, middle C in the bass clef.
6 Know the importance of 'landmarks' and relationships of movement of notes (skips, steps) as useful aids in reading music.

Answers

EXERCISE 2.4

C F G E F D G F D

EXERCISE 2.5

F A G C B G B F G

EXERCISE 2.6

TEST YOURSELF

1 What is the meaning of the word 'pitch'?

2 How many letters are there in the musical alphabet?

3 Do pitches become higher or lower in sound when moving to the right on the keyboard?

4 How are the keys arranged on a keyboard?

5 Describe the make-up of a staff.

6 Name the two clefs of the grand staff.

7 Which note sits on a short line between treble and bass clef?

8 What are the first five pitches of the treble clef, starting with middle C?

9 Name the first five pitches of the bass clef, moving down from middle C.

10 Describe a movement by step.

3

Melody

In Chapter 1, you learned how rhythms are formed by using various note values. Chapter 2 introduced pitches, showing their location on the keyboard and how they are written on the staff. You are now ready to study how rhythm and pitch are combined to form a melody.

Combining rhythm and pitch

A melody consists of an organized series of different pitches. They are given time values and arranged in a time signature. This is demonstrated in the two examples that follow. Example a) is just a long series of various notes, all written as semibreves (whole notes). In example b), the pitches have been divided into bars and given note values and a time signature. Even before listening to the examples, the second series of notes seems visually to make more sense than the first.

Exercise 3.1 (Listening)

Following the musical notation, listen to the two examples,
noticing how the series of pitches was turned into a melody.

Analysing melodies

Before you will be able to write an interesting melodic line, it is
necessary to know more about the relationship between rhythm
and pitch and how they work together when combined into
melodies. To do this, some samples will be analysed in detail.

Insight

I study every melody I come across by first reading the
pitches, noting the direction of movement and repetitions.
This continual practice at any level helps develop expertise,
and makes learning to read music much easier and quicker.

Exercise 3.2 (Written)

Two short melodies follow. They are each eight bars in length and
use the notes you have already learned in the treble clef – middle C,
D, E, F, G. Study each of the melodies, beginning with saying the
names of the notes. Next, notice the directions the notes move. Do
they move in steps or skips? Are there repetitions of small melodic
patterns? Jot down your ideas and compare them with mine found
at the end of the chapter.

Exercise 3.3 (Listening)

Listen to each melody in Exercise 3.2 as it is played on the CD. Try to follow the musical notation. Two bars of introduction are played before the melody begins. A background accompaniment is played with the melody to add interest.

Creating rhythms

In your analysis of the previous music, you should have noticed patterns in both the rhythm and the pitch. Although a creative activity, music is not just a collection of rhythms and pitches picked at random. Even a short piece of music needs to be carefully planned. In this section, you will begin composing your own music, starting with rhythm.

Insight

When first learning to compose music, it is best to use a simple, short rhythm and a narrow range of pitches. As your composing skills develop, expand little by little, perhaps turning four bars into eight.

Rhythms need to be interesting, but also need to be held together by a certain amount of repetition. The next exercise contains the first two bars of a four-bar rhythm. There are various ways to complete the last two bars.

The most obvious way would be to use an exact repeat of the rhythms used in the first two bars. I've composed a few other solutions. Listen to them on the CD.

Exercise 3.4 (Listening)

a) Exact repetition

b) Repetition of second bar rhythm

c) Second bar rhythm used in reverse in third bar

d) Second and fourth bar identical

Exercise 3.5 (Written and practical)

The first two bars have been completed in the examples that follow. Compose the final two bars for each one, then clap your completed rhythms.

a)

b)

c)

d)

Insight

I always give myself at least two bars of count before clapping a rhythm. If the basic pulse is not established and I am not feeling it, chances are that the rhythm will not be performed correctly.

Phrases

Just as written words have punctuation marks such as commas to help structure a sentence, music also uses a type of punctuation. The phrase is similar to a line of writing and is several bars long. In simple music, a phrase is usually two or four bars in length, but there is no set rule about how long a phrase should last. Phrases group together bars which contain a musical thought. They are notated by a long, curved line starting from the first note and ending at the last note of the phrase.

In example a) that follows, I have written four bars containing two phrases of two bars each. The first two bars have been given, but the last two need to be completed with notes in the treble clef of middle C, D, E, F and G. Examples b) and c) show two different solutions. In b), the first and third bars are the same, both in rhythm and pitch. Bars 2 and 4 use the same rhythm but different notes. The repetition of similar patterns helps hold the melody together. Think of the first two bars as a question and the last two as the answer. Example c) shows music which does not use repetition or patterns, either in rhythm or pitch. The melody seems to wander without direction, making it harder to remember once heard and the listener is left up in the air.

💿 Exercise 3.6 (Listening)

Turn on the CD and listen to the examples. Notice how example
b) is much better balanced and more musical than c).

Insight

> You might think your written music looks OK on paper. It
> may contain repetition as well as variety. The final judgement,
> however, should only be given after actually hearing it. You
> may be surprised!

Exercise 3. 7 (Written)

Practise composing answering phrases to these exercises. You have
been given the first two bars for each. Be sure to use patterns and
repetitions. Use only the notes of middle C, D, E, F and G in the
treble clef. Put all the stems upwards and remember to use proper
spacing between the notes.

What makes a good melody?

A good melodic line has a sense of direction called a melodic curve.
It should fit the mood of the music and help express the meaning
of any words present. There are different ways of writing a melody
with a feeling of direction. One way is to start at its lowest notes
and move upwards to the highest point. The opposite of this is to
start high and work downwards. Other melodies might start low,
move to a high point and return to end low. The opposite of this is

to start high, reach a low point and return for a high ending. Study the diagrams of these four different melodic curves.

> **Insight**
> When learning a piece of music, I find it helpful to hum the basic direction of the melody. This is especially useful if the work has a melody I am not familiar with. It is a good starting point!

a) Starting low and ending high

b) Starting high and ending low

c) Starting low, reaching a high point then ending low

d) Starting high, reaching a low point and ending high

Exercise 3.8 (Practical)

The following exercises will help in developing your aural and listening skills. There will be a demonstration before each exercise.

a) On the CD you will hear a series of pitches. After each pitch there will be a pause for you to sing the pitch. Use 'la' or any sound you feel comfortable singing.

b) You will hear several different groups of three pitches. After hearing each group of three, there will be a pause for you to sing the three pitches you have just heard.

c) The final exercise uses rhythm only. You will hear a short rhythm. Immediately following the rhythm, there is a gap for you to clap an answering rhythm. What your answer consists of is entirely up to you!

GOALS

1 *Analyse music, understanding the importance of repetition and patterns.*
2 *Compose short answering rhythms and melodies.*
3 *Define 'phrase'.*
4 *List four types of melodic curve.*
5 *Sing given pitches accurately.*
6 *Clap an answering rhythm to a given rhythm.*

Answers

EXERCISE 3.2

a) First bar moves upwards in steps.
   First and third bars are the same.

   Rhythm uses a mixture of o, ♩, ♪ notes.

b) Most of the melody is based on a small skip followed by a step.
   Bars 1 and 2 are the same as 5 and 6.

   Rhythm uses ♩ and ♪ notes.

3. Melody   31

TEST YOURSELF

1 *Rhythm and pitch are combined to form what?*

2 *What does a melody contain?*

3 *Although music needs to be interesting and creative, what is necessary to hold it together?*

4 *What is the easiest way to complete a four-bar rhythm with the first two bars given?*

5 *Give three other ways, based on the same four-bar rhythm.*

6 *What needs to be established before clapping a rhythm?*

7 *How is a phrase indicated?*

8 *Define a melodic curve.*

9 *What must a melodic curve fit?*

10 *If a melodic curve starts low, give two directions it might follow.*

4

More about pitch

In this chapter, the names of the notes for the rest of the staff, both treble and bass clef, are presented. It is important to learn to recognize these because much of the future work is based on being able to read notation quickly and accurately. The written exercises and listening will help you in this learning by repetition and reinforcement. The later part of the chapter deals with notation of stems, leger lines and clefs other than treble and bass.

The octave

The treble clef in the following example shows the five notes you have already learned. Added to these are three new ones – A, B, C. The higher C is one octave above middle C. An octave is a note whose letter-name is the repetition of the letter-name of another note. The octave note may be either higher or lower. The seven letter-names of the musical alphabet (the white keys on the keyboard) plus the repeated letter-name make the octave.

Treble clef with the notes in the C octave

Study the bass clef now. It also includes three new notes – E, D, C. The lower C is an octave below middle C. It may be helpful to locate the octave and new notes on the keyboard diagram in Chapter 2.

C B A G F E D C

Exercise 4.1 (Written)

This written work will give further practice in learning the notes you have studied so far. For the exercise, you need to write the letter-names under each of the notes. Use semibreves (whole notes) because this work deals with pitch only, not rhythm. Remember to think about how the notes move in relation to each other and your landmarks.

a)

C _ _ _ _ _ _ _ _ _

b)

G _ _ _ _ _ _ _ _ _

For more practice, you should write your own series of notes and identify them as you just have done.

Exercise 4.2 (Practical)

This exercise provides a chance to hear what you have been reading and writing about. It is designed to give listening practice in distinguishing the difference in sound between steps, skips and the octave. The step, one note moving to the next directly above or below it, is called a second. Examples are C up to D, E up to F, or E down to D. A small skip, leaving one note in between, is a third. Examples include C up to E, D up to F, or G down to E. Before starting your listening, locate these examples on the keyboard diagram. Don't worry about the black keys for the present.

When listening to the demonstration on the CD, notice that the second has a dissonant, rather harsh sound, but the third is consonant and more pleasing to the ear. The octave is easier to recognize as it contains a much larger skip. For the listening exercise which follows the demonstration, you will hear a series of pitches played in pairs, first sounded separately and then together. Each pair will be repeated three times before moving on to the next. You need to identify each pair as a second, third or octave. Jot down your answers and check them at the end of the chapter.

···
Insight
Listening to the different sounds of the step, skip and octave is a good way of learning. I find that actually humming or singing the sounds also helps in recogizing their differences.
···

Completing the notes on the staff

The rest of the notes for treble and bass clef come next. Notice that a line note becomes a space note in the next octave and a space note becomes a line note. Exercise 4.3 will help you learn them.

All the notes on the staff

Fill in the names of the pitches. Only the new notes just presented are used but treble and bass clef are both used.

a)

b)

> ## Insight
> From experience, I have found that learning the notes of the bass clef always seems to be more difficult than learning those of the treble clef. This might be because the letter-names do not follow the alphabet as clearly. To help your learning, set a goal of only learning a few new pitches at one time. It will make it less confusing.

Exercise 4.4 (Practical)

This exercise uses dictation to provide more practice in developing speed in reading music. On the CD you will hear descriptions of pitches to write on the staff. The first series will be for the treble clef, followed by a series for bass. Answers are at the end of the chapter.

a)

b)

Notation of stems

Look through the examples that follow and notice the directions of the stems. Some go upwards, while others go downwards. The general rule in music notation is that for any note with the head below the third line, the stem goes upwards. For any note above the third line, the stem goes downwards. If a note is on the third line, the stem may be placed in either direction to fit into the context. Writing stems in the correct direction keeps the music tidy and easy to read. Compare the two examples below to see the difference!

Leger (ledger) lines

Short lines drawn above or below the staff for notes which are pitched higher or lower are called leger (ledger) lines. Added lines do continue but become increasingly difficult to read.

Staff showing leger lines

Some notes may appear in both clefs written as leger lines. This happens particularly in piano/keyboard music. The example that follows shows a short piece of piano music written in two different ways. The first is for left hand only in bass clef, followed by the second for right hand in treble clef.

Study the pieces in the last two examples, making sure you understand the use of leger lines. Follow the written music while it is played on the CD. You will hear that both tunes sound exactly the same although they are notated differently.

OCTAVE SIGN – 8VA

Pitches may be written an octave lower or higher than they are meant actually to sound. This is done to make them easier to read by avoiding difficult leger lines. The octave sign, 8va, is marked over or under these notes. If it is written above, the notes will sound an octave higher. If it is written below, the notes will sound an octave lower.

Insight

As you have seen above, leger (ledger) lines are very difficult to read, but sometimes they do need to be used. When possible, though, it is best to use the easiest and clearest way of notating pitches, like the octave sign.

Other clefs

Besides the treble and bass clefs, there are other less commonly used clefs found in some music. The C clef, written 𝄡, is a moveable clef. This means that it can be placed in any position on the staff to mark a new location for middle C. When the C clef is on the middle line, it is called the alto clef, and when on the fourth line, it is called the tenor clef. Alto and tenor clefs are used mainly for music written for certain instruments such as viola, cello, bassoon and sometimes trombone.

Examples of alto and tenor clefs

Exercise 4.6 (Written)

Name the pitches below in alto and tenor clefs.

a)

b)

GOALS

1 *Define the term 'octave'.*
2 *Be able to read all the notes in treble and bass clefs.*
3 *Distinguish the difference in sound when hearing a step, skip and octave.*
4 *Understand the use of leger lines and the octave sign, 8va.*
5 *Understand the placement of pitches in alto and tenor clefs.*

Answers

EXERCISE 4.1

a) 𝄞 ^{middle}C G F B A C D F E C G

b) 𝄢 G C D F C E A B ^{middle}C G F

EXERCISE 4.2

2 3 8 3 2 8 8 3 2

EXERCISE 4.3

a) 𝄞 C G D E G F C D G F E

b) 𝄢 C G F A B C A G C B F

EXERCISE 4.4

a)

b)

EXERCISE 4.6

a) C E F G F B

b) C G A E F A

TEST YOURSELF

1 *What name is given to a note that repeats the letter-name of a lower note?*

2 *In treble clef, where is E located?*

3 *In bass clef, where is A located?*

4 *If the head of a note is below the third line of the staff, in which direction is the stem written?*

5 *If the head of a note is above the third line of the staff, in which direction is the stem written?*

6 *What if the head of the note has the third line running through it?*

7 *What are leger (ledger) lines?*

8 *Explain how the 8va sign is used.*

9 *Where is middle C located when the alto clef is used?*

10 *Where is middle C located on the tenor clef?*

5

More about rhythm

For the moment, let's leave pitch and melody and return to learning more about rhythm. This chapter introduces both new time signatures and new note values. There is a section explaining the time signature of $\frac{3}{4}$ and one on dotted notes and ties. Later parts of the chapter deal with other note values and less common time signatures. Demonstration, written and practical work are included to help in the learning process.

$\frac{3}{4}$ time

In the time signature of $\frac{3}{4}$, there are three beats in each bar. As in $\frac{2}{4}$ and $\frac{4}{4}$ time, the crotchet (quarter note) gets one beat. $\frac{3}{4}$ time is also known as waltz time. Another dance, the minuet, is also written in $\frac{3}{4}$. Study the following example. It shows that the first beat of each bar receives a slight accent.

Exercise 5.1 (Listening)

On the CD you will hear some examples using $\frac{3}{4}$ time. They will be played at various speeds. Listen for the strong first beat of each bar.

Dotted notes

Dotted notes are often found in ¾ time. A small dot placed after a note adds to it half the original value. A minim (half note) which last for two beats will be worth three beats when dotted. Rests may also be dotted. A dotted minim (half note) rest lasts for three beats.

Examples of dotted notes and rests

Tied notes

When a note is carried over into the following bar, a curved line called a tie is used. This makes the value of the original note longer because it is joined or tied to the next bar. The curved line is written between the note heads, not the stems. A tie has to be between two notes of the same pitch.

Example showing a tied note

There is no limit on the length of a tie.

Exercise 5.2 (Practical)

The following exercises are in ¾ time and are designed to give practical experience by clapping the rhythms. They include rests, dotted notes and ties. When clapping the exercises, keep your hands together to indicate a note is being held. On the CD you will hear two bars of count before you begin to clap. The correct rhythm will be played directly after your performance. Remember to look through the exercises before turning on the CD.

a) $\frac{3}{4}$ 1 2 3 | 1 2 3 | ♩ ♩ ♩ | ♩. | ♩ ♩ | ♩ ♩ ♩ ‖

b) $\frac{3}{4}$ 1 2 3 | 1 2 3 | ♩ ♩ | — | ♩ ♩ ♩ | ♩ ♩ ‖

c) $\frac{3}{4}$ 1 2 3 | 1 2 3 | ♩. | ♩ ♩ ♩ | ♩. | ♩ ♩ ‖

Exercise 5.3 (Written)

Add bar-lines to the following:

a) $\frac{3}{4}$ ♩ ♩ ♩ ♩ ♩ ♩ ♩ ♩ ♩. ♩. ♩ ♩ ‖

b) $\frac{3}{4}$ ♩ ♩ ♩ ♩ ♩ ♩ ♩ ♩ ♩ ♩ ♩ ♩ ♩ ♩. ‖

c) $\frac{3}{4}$ ♩ ♩ ♩ ♩ ♩ ♩ ♩ ♩ ♩. ♩. ♩. ♩ ♩ ‖

Insight

If you are finding it difficult to add the bar-lines, it is sometimes helpful to start from the end of the rhythm and work backwards. Warning! This does not always work. Later in this chapter, when you learn about incomplete bars, you will see why.

Try composing an eight-bar rhythm of your own. Use dotted notes, ties and rests to make it interesting. Clap your completed rhythm, using a speed you are able to keep steady.

$\frac{3}{4}$ | | | | | | | ‖

Quavers (eighth notes)

You have seen how in $\frac{2}{4}$, $\frac{3}{4}$ and $\frac{4}{4}$ time the crotchet (quarter note) receives one beat. The quaver (eighth note), however, only lasts for half of one beat in these time signatures, so it becomes necessary to divide each beat into parts smaller than one. Before going any further into counting quavers, let's study how they are written. Quavers are written individually with an added tail to the stem. The tail is always added on the right side. They are also joined together by a beam. If there are several quavers (eighth notes) in a row, it is easier to read them if they are grouped together.

Examples of quavers

Sometimes, there may be groups of four or more quavers beamed together. In $\frac{4}{4}$ time, they should never be beamed across the middle of the bar, as there needs to be a clear indication of where the third beat starts.

Wrong	**Correct**

The quaver (eighth note) also has a rest written as 𝄾.

COUNTING QUAVERS

There are two quavers (eighth notes) to every crotchet (quarter note) beat, making the quaver worth half a beat. When first learning to count these, it is best to say 'and' between the beats. This helps you place the quaver (eighth note) evenly between the beats. It may be helpful to count 'and' continuously throughout each bar to keep a steady beat. The quavers (eighth notes) will easily fall into place when they occur.

1 & 2 & 3 & 4 &   1 & 2 & 3 & 4 &

Insight

Even before you begin to practise a rhythm that uses quavers or eighth notes, just chant 1 & 2 & 3 & 4 & over and over until it becomes second nature. If you are stumbling over the words, your clapping will suffer.

Exercise 5.4 (Practical)

Look through the exercises that follow. They use quavers, rests and ties. The first one will be demonstrated for you, with two bars of introductory count. Try clapping the rest of the exercises. You will hear the correct rhythm played directly after the space left for your performance. Remember to check the time signatures!

a)

b)

c)

DOTTED CROTCHETS

A dot placed after a crotchet (quarter note) adds to it half its original value, which equals a quaver (eighth note). The dotted crotchet therefore lasts for one and a half beats.

Exercise 5.5 (Listening)

Listen to the three examples on the CD. They will be played once with counting, followed by once without.

a)

b)

c)

EXERCISE

In this exercise, you will hear a backing track for the Cuban dance known as the Cha Cha. You are going to join in by clapping a rhythm called the clave. Before turning on the CD, practise the clave rhythm.

Clave rhythm

1 & 2 & 3 & 4 &   1 & 2 & 3 & 4 &   (repeat)

Semiquavers (sixteenth notes)

When you studied quavers (eighth notes) in the previous section, it was explained that their value was half of one beat. Notes with values shorter than quavers (eighth notes) are sometimes used. A semiquaver (sixteenth note) lasts only half as long as a quaver (eighth note). The next examples show how semiquavers (sixteenth notes) are written and counted. You may find it helpful to count each semiquaver as shown here.

Examples of semiquavers

1 e & e

(grouped together as one beat)

Rest

Semiquavers (sixteenth notes) may also be mixed and joined to notes of other values. Study the examples that follow, two of which show the dotted quaver (eighth note) joined to a semiquaver (sixteenth note). The dotted quaver is equal to three semiquavers.

a) 1 e & e 2 e & e 3 e & e 4 e & e

b)

c)

Insight

For learning to count semiquavers or sixteenth notes, practise saying 1 e & e 2 e & e 3 e & e 4 e & e until the words flow naturally. It may seem silly to dwell on making these sounds, but if you don't, your performance will suffer, especially as the rhythms become more difficult.

Exercise 5.7 (Practical)

Try clapping these last three rhythms, keeping your clapping even and steady.

DEMI-SEMIQUAVER (THIRTY-SECOND NOTE)

There is one other note value which should be mentioned, the demi-semiquaver (thirty-second note). It lasts only half as long as the semiquaver (sixteenth note). You will not find demi-semiquavers used very often unless you are performing fairly difficult music.

Examples of demi-semiquavers (thirty-second notes)

 Rest

Triplets

As you have already seen with the quaver, a beat can be split into two equal parts.

When a beat is divided into three equal parts, it is notated as a triplet. A small number 3 is written over or under the three notes, and many times a curved line or bracket is added. If it is a crotchet (quarter note) beat being divided into three, the three notes in the triplet are written as quavers (eighth notes).

Listen to the following examples using triplets, performed on the CD.

Insight

In order to gain more practice with triplets, try clapping the rhythms given in Exercise 5.8. After you feel sure of yourself, turn your CD back on and clap along with the recording. Actually performing helps in the learning process.

Other less commonly used time signatures

In the following table, you will find some of the less commonly used time signatures.

2 Two beats in each bar 2 Minim (half note) gets one beat	2 2 ♩ ♩ | ♩ ♩ ‖ 1 2 1 2
4 Four beats in each bar 2 Minim (half note) gets one beat	4 2 ♩ ♩ ♩ ♩ | ♩ ♩ ♩ ♩ ‖ 1 2 3 4 1 2 3 4

3 Three beats in each bar 8 Quaver (eighth note) gets one beat		
9 Nine beats in each bar 8 Quaver (eighth note) gets one beat		
12 Twelve beats in each bar 8 Quaver (eighth note) gets one beat		

Incomplete bars

A piece of music may begin with a bar containing fewer than the required number of beats stated in the time signature. The notes in the incomplete bars are often referred to as an anacrusis or as pick-up notes. The following example shows music written in $\frac{4}{4}$. There are only three beats in the first bar, but the last bar contains only one beat. Adding the notes of the first and last bars together equals four beats. Examples of popular tunes that start with an incomplete bar include 'Happy birthday' and 'Oh when the saints go marching in'.

Examples of music beginning with incomplete bars

Syncopation

When an expected accent is displaced, rhythms occur where usually weak beats are given strong accents. This is called syncopation and is used in various styles of music, particularly ragtime.

> **Insight**
>
> Syncopated rhythms are often very hard to learn. This is because the weak beats you have become accustomed to are now strong. One way to develop a feeling for syncopation is to continually practise clapping or playing it. How about starting with the two rhythms given above?

GOALS

1 Understand ¾ time, including dotted and tied notes.
2 Be able to count quavers (eighth notes).
3 Understand dotted crotchets (dotted quarter notes).
4 Play a rhythm which includes quavers along with the CD.
5 Count and notate semiquavers (sixteenth notes) and triplets.
6 Know the counting of less common time signatures.
7 Understand incomplete bars and syncopation.

Answers

EXERCISE 5.3

a)

b)

c)

TEST YOURSELF

1 *What is another name for $\frac{3}{4}$ time?*

2 *How many beats per bar in waltz time?*

3 *What is placed after a note to increase its original value by half?*

4 *What is a tied note?*

5 *How many counts does a quaver or eighth note get in $\frac{3}{4}$ time?*

6 *Compare the note values of a quaver or eighth note to a semiquaver or sixteenth note.*

7 *Describe a triplet.*

8 *What type of note gets the beat in $\frac{3}{8}$ time?*

9 *If a piece of music begins with a bar containing fewer than the required number of beats shown in the time signature, what is that bar called?*

10 *What is syncopation?*

6

Sharps and flats

Sharps and flats are important signs in musical notation. They are used to raise or lower pitches. The structures of key signatures scales and chords all involve the use of sharps and flats. A clear understanding is therefore needed before moving on to study these topics. Locating sharps and flats on the keyboard provides a good visual starting point.

Sharps and flats on the keyboard

When studying the layout of the keyboard in Chapter 2, the black keys were used as 'landmarks' for locating the white keys. The diagram below shows how the black keys get their names from the white.

If a black key is higher in pitch than the white key, i.e. located a semitone (half tone) to the right of it, it is called 'sharp'. If, instead,

the black key is located to the left of the white, it is called 'flat'.
Sharps and flats do not always involve black keys. For example,
'C flat' is the same as B and 'F flat' is E. The two different names
for the same pitch are called an enharmonics.

Insight

Exercise 6.1 below only gives you a small amount of practice in
locating keys up and down the keyboard. It is really important
to be able to find keys quickly if you are going to be successful
with future chapters. To gain more practice, write out your
own series similar to the exercise and locate them.

Exercise 6.1 (Written)

On the keyboard diagram in Chapter 2, locate the following keys
up and down the keyboard. Underneath each, write the name of
the enharmonic.

A♭ B♭ C♯ E♭ G♯ D♭ F♭ C♭ D♯ B A♯

G♯ __ __ __ __ __ __ __ __ __ __

Notation for sharps and flats

There are musical signs to show when a pitch is to be raised or
lowered.

♯ is sharp   ♭ is flat

When writing a sharp or flat sign beside a note, the sign must be
placed before the note and on the same line or space.

Practise adding sharps and flats to the following notes, then write the letter-name under each. The sign goes before the note on the staff but after the letter-name! This exercise is a good review for reading pitches in both treble and bass clef.

Insight

Be careful when writing out your answers. Notating music correctly is very important. I remember being marked down on an assignment at college because of sloppy notation. Anything my tutor wasn't clear about was counted as wrong!

Accidentals

When a composer wants to alter an individual pitch in a work, a sharp or flat sign is written as needed. These are called accidentals. Once an accidental has been added, it remains 'active' for the rest of that bar. If a note has been made sharp or flat but the composer then wants to return to the original pitch within that same bar, a natural sign, ♮, must be used. A bar-line automatically cancels an accidental, so it must be added again if required in the next bar. Note that an accidental only applies to the pitch of the note to which it has been added. If, for example, a sharp has been added to an F on the first space of the treble clef and there is a higher F in the same bar, a sharp must be added to the higher F as well.

Example showing adding accidentals to notes of the same name but of different pitches

Insight

For practice in recognizing accidentals in the context of a piece of music, find a variety of printed music and have a look through. Try to spot all of the added sharps, flats and natural signs. This is a good music reading exercise!

Exercise 6.3 (Listening)

Study the tune 'Accidental blues'. It is a 12-bar blues, a popular form used in jazz. In blues music, there are many altered pitches called 'blues notes'. These add tension and feeling, helping to set the mood of the music. Listen to 'Accidental blues' on the CD. The notes are arranged in bass and treble clef and split between left and right hands when played on piano or keyboard. See if you are able to follow the notes.

'Accidental blues'

Double sharps and double flats

There are some occasions when a note already sharpened will be raised yet again. This is called a double sharp, the sign being a cross ✗. In the example that follows, the double sharp changes the C♯ to C✗. The enharmonic pitch is D. Double sharps function as accidentals and affect all the notes of the same pitch for the rest of the bar unless cancelled. There are different ways of cancelling a double sharp. One way is just to write one sharp in front of the pitch. Another way is to write a natural sign plus one sharp.

Examples of cancelling double sharps

A double flat, written ♭♭, lowers a pitch which is already flattened. As with double sharps, the sign is added as an accidental and lasts throughout the bar unless cancelled.

Examples of cancelling double flats

Make the following into double sharps or double flats, then write
the name of the enharmonic below each one.

Insight

Don't be afraid of those double sharps and double flats!
Being a musician since an early age, I haven't come across
them too often. To see them in context, study some difficult
printed music for piano. You may be able to spot a few.

GOALS

1 *Locate sharps and flats on the keyboard.*
2 *Correctly notate sharps and flats on the staff.*
3 *Understand the rules for adding and cancelling accidentals.*
4 *Understand adding and cancelling double sharps and
   double flats.*

Answers

EXERCISE 6.1

EXERCISE 6.2

🎼 G♯ E♯ F♯ C♯ A♯ D♯ B♭ D♭ E♭ G♭ A♭ D♭

𝄢 C♯ F♯ A♯ E♯ G♯ D♯ B♯ D♭ E♭ C♭ A♭ G♭ C♭

EXERCISE 6.4

F♯ G B♭ A D♯ E G♭ F C♯ D

G♭ F G♯ A A♭ G E♭ D C♯ D

TEST YOURSELF

1 On the piano keyboard, if a black key is located a semitone or half tone to the right of the white key, is it sharp or flat?

2 When writing a sharp or flat beside a note, where must it be placed?

3 What is the term for sharp, flat and natural signs?

4 How long is an accidental 'active'?

5 When a letter-name is used to identify a pitch, where is the accidental written?

6 What automatically cancels an accidental?

7 If a sharp is added to F on the first space in treble clef, will this automatically apply to any F in that bar?

8 Sometimes an already sharpened note needs to be raised again. What is this called?

9 What is an already flattened note called if it is flattened again?

10 Name the enharmonic of A double flat.

7

Intervals

An interval is the distance between two pitches and may be large or small. It is important to have a thorough understanding and working knowledge of intervals, as scale and chord construction, which will be studied later in this book, are based on arrangements of intervals. Also, being able to quickly recognize how written intervals sound helps in sight reading and in following musical scores. This chapter will help you understand about writing intervals, as well as recognizing their different sounds. It would be helpful to have the keyboard diagram handy while studying intervals.

Semitones and whole tones

The closest distance in pitch between two notes is the semitone or half tone. Examples are C moving up to D♭ or F♯ moving up to G. On the keyboard, a semitone is not necessarily a white key moving to a black. E to F is a semitone, as is B to C. There are no black keys between E and F or B and C. The interval made of two semitones is called a whole tone or simply a tone. C moving up to D is a tone, comprising C to D♭ (semitone) and D♭ to D (semitone). Intervals may be built either upwards or downwards from a given note.

Exercise 7.1 (Written)

The following is a series of semibreves (whole notes). Some are in treble clef, others are in bass. For the first group, draw the note which

(Contd)

EXERCISE

is a semitone higher than the given note, and write the letter-names of both notes. Remember that an interval shows the distance between two notes. A semitone above G, for example, can be written as either G♯ or A♭. However, when identifying intervals, use the notation that shows movement from one note to another, in this case, the A♭.

a)

For this group, draw the note which is a semitone lower than the given note. Follow the rest of the instructions as already given.

b)

For the final group, draw the note a whole tone higher than the given note, then name both notes. Warning: the intervals between E to F and B to C are tricky.

c)

Insight

It is always helpful to actually hear what you have written. If you have a piano or electronic keyboard available, try playing some semitones or half tones up and down the keys. For further practice in reading notation, you might try playing your written answers from above.

Other intervals

There are five different types of interval: major, minor, perfect, augmented and diminished. The major and perfect intervals will be explained first. The name of an interval is determined by the number of scale steps involved and the relationship to the first note, the keynote. A unison is a note of the same pitch as the starting note.

Because intervals involve the space between two notes, two separate parts need to be notated to show this. In the next example, middle C, is the keynote. The other intervals are counted from C, which is number 1. The intervals of the fourth, fifth and octave are called perfect intervals, abbreviated as P. The second, third, sixth and seventh are major intervals with the abbreviation of M.

| Unison | M2 | M3 | P4 | P5 | M6 | M7 | Octave |

....
Insight

Learning to recognize intervals is a skill necessary for sight reading and sight singing. A good practice exercise involves humming any pitch as a keynote, then counting up to another pitch and humming that one. 'Signature tunes' help. The sound of an upward perfect fifth is the beginning of 'Twinkle, twinkle little star'!
....

Each interval contains a certain number of semitones from the keynote. The table that follows shows the number of semitones which make up each interval, counting upwards from the keynote. When constructing an interval, always count the keynote as one. You can find any interval above a given note by counting the semitones upwards from this given note.

Interval	
Major second	2 semitones
Major third	4
Perfect fourth	5
Perfect fifth	7
Major sixth	9
Major seventh	11

Exercise 7.2 (Written)

Counting upwards from the bottom note, which acts as the keynote for each, construct the interval above the given note. Some intervals will require the addition of a sharp or flat as shown in the example to make the number of semitones required for the interval correct.

a) M3 P4 P5 M3 M2 P4 M6 M7 M3 M6 P5

b) P4 P4 P5 M3 P4 M6 M7 M2 M2 M3 M7

Exercise 7.3 (Listening and practical)

On the CD, you will hear a demonstration of the sounds of different intervals found within the octave. Helpful information will be given as to how to recognize different intervals. Listen to the intervals played on the CD. Each will be repeated three times. You need to write down the interval you think you heard. This gives practice in recognizing the sounds of various intervals and is especially helpful in sight reading or sight singing.

Insight

As you now have a variety of intervals to identify, you'll probably need to find your own 'signature tunes' to use as prompts. Another favourite of mine is 'Here comes the bride' for an upward perfect fourth such as C up to F.

Minor, diminished and augmented intervals

A major interval becomes minor by lowering the top note one semitone or raising the bottom note that same distance. If it is made another semitone smaller, the interval then becomes diminished.

Examples of minor and diminished intervals

Perfect intervals become diminished if made a semitone smaller. They do not become minor.

Examples of perfect intervals made diminished

Major and perfect intervals become augmented intervals if expanded by one semitone. The augmented fourth/diminished fifth is known as the tritone because it contains three whole tones. Until the 20th century, the tritone was considered to be a particularly dissonant and restless interval which needed to be used carefully, having the tension it created properly resolved.

The example that follows shows minor, diminished and augmented intervals using middle C as the keynote. Notice that the augmented fourth and diminished fifth are the same, as are the augmented fifth and minor sixth. These are called enharmonic intervals. Don't worry about diminished and augmented seconds, thirds, sixths and sevenths. These are very rarely used.

The following table shows the number of semitones contained in minor, diminished and augmented intervals.

Interval	
Minor second	1 semitone
Minor third	3
Diminished fourth	4
Augmented fourth	6
Diminished fifth	6
Augmented fifth	8
Minor sixth	8
Minor seventh	10

Exercise 7.4 (Written)

The following is a series of major intervals. Change them to minor by adding the necessary accidentals to the upper note.

a)

M3 Mi3 M6 Mi6 M2 Mi2 M7 Mi7 M3 Mi3

Now change the following perfect intervals to diminished or augmented as indicated.

b)

P4 Aug4 P5 Dim5 P5 Dim5 P4 Dim4

Exercise 7.5 (Listening and practical)

First listen to examples of minor, augmented and diminished intervals. A series will then be played for you to identify the type of interval. Jot down your answers as you listen.

Inverted intervals

An interval may be inverted by moving the lower note an octave higher or the higher note an octave lower. When inverted, a perfect interval remains perfect, but a major interval becomes minor and a diminished interval becomes augmented. The original number of the interval and the number of its inversion always add up to nine. In the following examples, a) shows the lower note moved to the top, while b) shows the higher note moved to the bottom.

a)

b)

Compound intervals

Compound intervals are larger than an octave. The interval of a ninth is an octave plus a second (one step). An octave plus a third (two steps) is called a tenth. Beyond the interval of a tenth, the octave may not be counted, so an 11th is called a compound fourth, and a 12th is called a compound fifth.

Examples of compound intervals

M9   M10   Mi10

GOALS

1 *Define the term 'interval'.*
2 *Know the difference between a semitone and a whole tone.*
3 *Construct intervals above a given keynote.*
4 *Recognize the sounds of different intervals found within an octave (e.g. second, third, fourth).*
5 *Be able to write and recognize when played, the different types of interval (i.e. major, minor, augmented and diminished).*
6 *Understand inverted and compound intervals.*

Answers

EXERCISE 7.1

b)

| A | G♯ | | E | D♯ | | G | F♯ | | B | A♯ | | D | C♯ |

| C | B | | F | E | | C | B | | E | D♯ | | D | C♯ |

c)

| G | A | | C | D | | C | D | | F | G | | D | E |

| D | E | | E | F♯ | | D | E | | G | A | | E | F♯ |

EXERCISE 7.2

a) M3 P4 P5 M3 M2 P4 M6 M7 M3 M6 P5

b) P4 P4 P5 M3 P4 M6 M7 M2 M2 M3 M7

EXERCISE 7.3

P4 M3 M2 Octave P5 M3 P4 M6 M7

EXERCISE 7.4

a) M3 Mi3 M6 Mi6 M2 Mi2 M7 Mi7 M3 Mi3

b) P4 Aug4 P5 Dim5 P5 Dim5 P4 Dim4

TEST YOURSELF

1 What is the closest distance between two pitches called?

2 How many semitones or half tones are in a whole tone?

3 Give the name of the pitch located a whole tone above A.

4 The intervals of the fourth, fifth and octave are of which type?

5 How many semitones or half tones does a major sixth contain?

6 If a minor interval is made smaller, what type of interval does it become?

7 What if a perfect interval is made smaller?

8 How many semitones or half tones are there in a minor third?

9 Explain two ways an interval may be inverted.

10 Give an example of a compound interval.

8

More about intervals

In the previous chapter, you learned about the construction of individual intervals and how they sound when played together. These are harmonic intervals. In this chapter you will discover how intervals are linked together in music to form complete melodies. These are melodic intervals.

🔾 Exercise 8.1 (Listening and written)

Look at the following short melody of eight bars, written in treble clef. Listen to it on the CD, following the notes as the tune is played. After your listening, mark the intervals between the notes with brackets. Some move upwards from the previous note, others downwards. For further practice, this exercise can be carried out on any piece of music.

EXERCISE

Sight reading

Sight reading is a skill which needs continuous practice. It involves being able to look at a piece of written music and know what it sounds like and then performing it, even before hearing it performed. There are different ways to approach a tune you want to sight read. The following exercise will take you through some of the steps.

Exercise 8.2 (Practical)

The following tune is a familiar one and you should be able to identify it by studying it in various ways. First, quickly look through the piece, noticing the clef, time signature and any added sharps or flats. Try clapping the rhythm, then analysing the way the notes move. The first three notes in this tune are repeats of C. These are followed by a step moving upwards and two more repeated notes. See if you can sing the first eight bars of the melody. You might use 'la' or the letter-names of the notes. Check the name of the tune at the end of the chapter before moving on to the next exercise.

> **Insight**
>
> For more practice in sight reading, pick some easy folk songs. Follow the steps given in Exercise 8.2. Even if you know the name of the song, it is still helpful to practise the steps until you get to the point where you use them instinctively.

Transposing

Transposing involves moving all the notes of a piece of music the same distance up or down. It is used to put music into a range which is more comfortable for a player or singer. Transposing a melody up or down an octave is fairly easy because the names of the notes stay the same.

Insight

It's all well and good to think you understand the process of transposition. However, if you still are not clear about identifying intervals, chances are you may start your transposition on the wrong pitch. Everything following that note will also be wrong!

Exercise 8.3 (Written)

Transpose 'Row, row, row' up one octave from bass clef to treble clef.

Figure 8.3.

Now transpose it up the interval of a perfect fourth from your version in treble clef. Check your starting note with the back of the chapter before completing the entire transposition.

⊙ Exercise 8.4 (Listening)

Listen to 'Row, row, row' played, transposed in different ways.

⊙ Exercise 8.5 (Practical)

How many times have you wished you could write down a melody
you have heard in music notation? This exercise will show you the
basics of how to do this by using melodic dictation. There follow
skeletons for two short melodies of four bars each. On the CD,
each melody will be played five times. There will be a pause after
each repetition to give you a chance to write down what you have
heard. Try to listen for intervals you recognize in the melody. On
each listening, it is best to try to get something written down for
every bar, adding more on each repetition.

a)

b)

76

Insight

It is very easy to get flustered when first learning to take musical dictation. There are rhythms and pitches galore, and you know you only have a few chances to write them down correctly. Do try to focus on one element at a time, perhaps jotting down the rhythm first.

GOALS

1 *Be able to analyse the intervals of a melody line.*
2 *Know the steps for sight reading music.*
3 *Understand basic transposition.*
4 *Write down a simple melody from music dictation.*

Answers

EXERCISE 8.1
a) M3   b) M2   c) P4   d) P5   e) M2   f) Mi3   g) Mi3   h) M3

EXERCISE 8.2
'Row, row, row your boat'.

EXERCISE 8.3
Starting note first space F; a perfect fourth above middle C.

EXERCISE 8.5

a)

b)

TEST YOURSELF

1 *What are melodic intervals?*

2 *In a melodic line, name the interval of G moving up to C.*

3 *Name the melodic interval of D moving down to G.*

4 *What is sight reading?*

5 *How would you analyse a melody in sight reading?*

6 *What is transposing?*

7 *What happens if you forget to transpose a pitch?*

8 *If you were to transpose a melody a perfect fifth up from C, on which note would the new melody start?*

9 *What if you wanted to transpose a melody a whole tone below D? Where would it start?*

10 *When listening to melodic dictation, should you wait until you have heard the whole melody several times, or jot down a little after each hearing?*

9

Major scales and key signatures

Introduction to different types of scale

A scale is the alphabetical succession of notes beginning on a particular pitch. The word is derived from the Latin *scala*, which means a ladder. All music is composed using some form of scale. Many different types of scale have been used in music through the ages, from ancient church modes, folk music of different lands to the innovative 12-note row devised in the 20th century. Scales sound different from one another because of the way the pitches are arranged. In medieval music, the various scale formations were called modes, each having its own individual arrangement of whole tones and semitones. We will begin the study of scales by listening to some examples on the CD.

Exercise 9.1 (Listening)

This exercise is designed to give you a general idea of the sounds of different modes. Try to follow the notation as you listen to each example as it is played on the keyboard.

(Contd)

EXERCISE

Insight

The chromatic scale is constructed by using semitones or half tones only. There is no 'keynote'. All of the intervals are equal. Listening to the chromatic scale provides really good practice in recognizing semitones or half tones because it isolates and continually repeats that interval.

Major scale construction

For approximately the past 400 years, most music in the Western world has used major or minor scales, the old medieval modes of Ionian and Aeolian. This chapter will deal with the major scale, first looking at how it is constructed.

A major scale is a series of semitones and whole tones arranged in a specific order. It is this arrangement that identifies it as major in sound. The notes for a C major scale can be found by playing just the white keys from any C to the C an octave higher. The notes contained in a scale are called degrees, with the starting note, the keynote, defining the tonal centre or key. Music using the scale of C major is referred to as being in the key of C or just 'in C'.

The following example shows the C major scale with degree numbers marked.

By analysing the intervals between the degrees, we find that there is a mixture of whole tones and semitones.

C to D is a whole tone
D to E is a whole tone
E to F is a semitone
F to G is a whole tone
G to A is a whole tone
A to B is a whole tone
B to C is a semitone.

The abbreviations used are T = tone or whole tone, and S = semitone. The pattern of T T S T T T S has emerged. The eight notes of a major scale may be divided into two sections of four notes each. Each section contains a tetrachord. The semitones occur at the same place in each tetrachord.

CONSTRUCTING OTHER MAJOR SCALES

The pattern set by the C major scale must be followed in constructing all major scales. Any note may be used as the starting or keynote, but C is the only major scale not needing any alterations to the white notes of the keyboard. A major scale starting on any other note will have changes made to the spacing. The intervals are made correct by adding either sharps or flats where needed.

The example that follows shows the construction of a major scale beginning on G. The interval between the E and F is only a semitone. A whole tone is needed at the point. Raising the F to F♯ creates a whole tone. The F♯ also makes a semitone between the F and G as required by the pattern.

Exercise 9.2 (Written)

This exercise gives you further practice in constructing major scales. See if you are able to construct major scales beginning and ending on F, A, B♭ and E. Remember to follow the pattern of T T S T T T S. It remains the same for all major scales, even if the starting note begins on a sharp or flat. Since the C major scale is the only major scale having no sharps or flats, some changes will be needed in the other series to make them fit the pattern. Either sharps or flats are used, depending on what needs to be altered.

Key signatures

The information at the beginning of a work showing sharps or flats is called the key signature. The only note altered in the series of notes from G to G was the F. It became F♯, which is the key signature for the key of G major. In this instance, the ♯ is written at the beginning of the piece to indicate that all Fs throughout the work will be sharp, whether pitched high or low. The key signature is repeated at the beginning of every line of music, unlike the time signature, which only appears once at the start of a work. Note that the F♯ cannot be written as a G♭. This would make two Gs (G and G♭) in the scale and no F. Each degree of the scale must be present.

Key signature for G major

Any key signature will use either sharps or flats. They are never mixed. You won't see a signature like this example. If you do, it's wrong!

Notation of key signatures

Wrong   Correct – using   Correct – using
flats only   sharps only

Insight

Careful and accurate notation of sharps and flats is just as
important as writing notes neatly. Practise drawing a few
sharps and flats, following the examples on page 56. The
staff lines either need to go through the middle of the sharps
and flats, or the signs need to be placed evenly in the spaces
between the lines.

Exercise 9.3 (Written)

This exercise shows the difference between adding accidentals and
writing key signatures. You may be asked to write a scale and add
the alterations (accidentals) to the series of notes. If this is the case, do
not write the key signature at the beginning. Using both is wrong. To
help in learning the pattern of a major scale, mark all the semitones.
Complete the following scales, carefully following the instructions:

a) *Write a scale from G to G, ascending. Include the key
    signature at the beginning.*

b) *Write a scale from D to D, ascending. Add accidentals to the
    degrees of the scale where needed.*

c) *Write a scale, descending from E, with the key signature included.*

d) *Write a scale, both ascending and descending, starting and ending on E♭, with the key signature included.*

The circle of fifths

It is not necessary to memorize all the key signatures. The circle of fifths is an easy way to find a key signature (see the diagram below).

For keys having sharps in the signature, start with C, located at the top. Move clockwise to G which has one sharp. Move on to D. There is an interval of a fifth between, or seven semitones. Each new key is five letter-names higher than the last, but be sure to count the semitones because some keys begin on a sharp or flat. For flat keys, read the circle anti-clockwise.

Listen to a demonstration of the circle of fifths.

Writing key signatures

Sharps and flats always appear in the same order, the new one added to the ones already there. Study the examples of how sharps and flats are written in both the treble and bass clefs. To learn the correct order, it might be helpful to copy them a few times. A chart containing key signatures is included in the back of the book for future reference.

Using the circle of fifths, write the key signatures for the following major keys:

GOALS

1 Name the medieval modes and their starting notes.
2 Understand how to construct a major scale.
3 Define 'key signature'.
4 Be able to find major key signatures by using the circle of fifths.
5 Know how to write sharps and flats as key signatures in the correct order.

Answers

EXERCISE 9.2

EXERCISE 9.3

a) G major scale

b) D major scale

c) E major scale

d) E♭ major scale

EXERCISE 9.5

TEST YOURSELF

1 Define a scale.

2 What makes scales sound different from each other?

3 Medieval scales are called what?

4 Write out the pattern for the construction of a major scale using T and S.

5 What are the notes contained in a scale called?

6 If a major scale begins on D, what alterations to the white notes of the keyboard need to be made to make the degrees fit the major scale pattern?

7 What is the key signature of A major?

8 Using the circle of fifths, find the key signature of E major.

9 If you are writing out the degrees of a scale, is it correct to add both the key signature and accidentals?

10 Name the order of the first three flats of a key signature.

10

Minor scales and key signatures

As well as the major scale, the minor is also commonly used in Western music. This chapter explores the minor, starting by comparing its construction with the major scale. Listening and written work help in understanding the three different forms of minor scales and minor key signatures. Parallel and relative minor signatures are also covered.

Minor scale construction

Just as C to C produced the pattern for major scales, A to A played on the white notes of the keyboard produces the pattern for the minor. Whereas the major scale has only one form, the minor has three: natural, harmonic and melodic. The A to A scale is the natural form, but the harmonic and melodic forms are more commonly found in music.

Minor scale in natural form

For the harmonic minor, the seventh degree is raised one semitone, both ascending and descending. In melodic, the sixth and seventh degrees are raised one semitone when ascending, but cancelled when descending, returning to the natural form. The alterations are added as accidentals where needed throughout the music.

The forms of minor scale used may vary within a piece with both the notes of the harmonic and melodic appearing. Because of this, music is said to be in a minor key, not harmonic or melodic minor.

Exercise 10.1 (Listening)

Listen to a demonstration of minor scales. The three different forms follow here.

....

Insight

You will need to listen to the examples of the three forms of minor scales many times as the changes are very subtle. Warning! Before listening, make sure you are clear about the differences in construction between the three!

....

Natural, harmonic and melodic forms

As with major scales, the minor in its natural form is also constructed using a series of semitones and whole tones. Their arrangement, however, is slightly different from the major scale pattern.

By analysing the intervals in the following example, the natural minor scale pattern can be found.

A to B is a whole tone
B to C is a semitone
C to D is a whole tone
D to E is a whole tone
E to F is a semitone
F to G is a whole tone
G to A is a whole tone.

The pattern for constructing a natural minor scale is T S T T S T T.

Exercise 10.2 (Written)

Using the pattern, construct a natural minor scale beginning on E. Add any accidentals needed to alter the intervals.

Which note would be raised to make the harmonic minor? (Remember, it is the same both ascending and descending.)

Write the melodic minor scale here, both ascending and descending, adding accidentals.

Before moving on, complete the following questions:

a) *Write a harmonic minor scale, ascending and descending, starting on the given note. Use a key signature.*

b) *Write a melodic minor scale, ascending and descending, starting on the given note. Use accidentals only.*

Insight

Following the example of Exercise 10.2, write out more starting pitches for practice. Be sure you are clear about the instructions as to whether to add accidentals only or to use a key signature. If you are confused by just one instruction, your entire exercise could turn out wrong!

Key signatures

As with the major scales, we can use a relationship of a fifth for finding minor key signatures.

Starting at the A which has no sharps or flats, read clockwise to find the signature for keys containing sharps, anti-clockwise for flats.

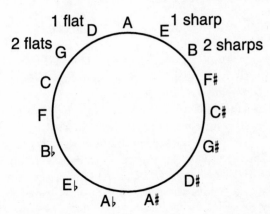

Using the circle of fifths, write the key signatures for the following minor keys:

C minor   F minor   B minor

G minor   B♭ minor   F♯ minor

Insight

From experience, I have found that students have more trouble learning minor key signatures than major. Keep drilling yourself on finding the minor by using the diagram of the circle of fifths. You can check your answers on the table of key signatures on page 197.

Parallel and relative minor key signatures

Minor key signatures relate to the major in two different ways: parallel and relative. C major and C minor are parallel. They have the same letter-name but different key signatures. C major has no sharps or flats but C minor has three flats. Relative keys have the same key signature but different letter-names. C major has no sharps or flats and A minor has no sharps or flats. If you know the major key signatures, it is easy to find a parallel minor key signature. For example, to find the parallel minor signature for C major, count up three semitones from C. This brings you to E♭. The key signature for E♭ major is three flats, the same as C minor!

Exercise 10.4 (Written)

Write the parallel key signatures for each of the following keys:

a)

D   D mi   A   A mi   B   B mi

b)

F   F mi   B♭   B♭ mi   C♯   C♯ mi

THE BLUES SCALE

The blues scale was introduced to you at the beginning of the chapter on major scales. It is a hybrid scale, being a major scale with a lowered third and seventh. These alterations are made to add feeling and emotion to blues music.

Example of major scale with 'blues' alterations

Insight

Listening to just one example of the 'blues' scale is not enough to give you a clear idea of its sound. See if you can find some recordings of 'blues'. (The word is usually in the title of the song.) Be aware of the deep emotions and feelings in the music.

Exercise 10.5 (Listening)

Finally, to end the two chapters on scales, I have composed a short tune called 'Fishy scales'. Within the piece, I have used several types of scales, some of which were introduced to you at the beginning of the chapter on major scales. These have been marked on your music. Listen for the differences.

(Contd)

'Fishy scales'

C major — C major

C minor — C minor

C major — C major

Chromatic

Dorian — Phrygian

C major

Insight

For further practice in identifying different types of scales, study as many pieces as possible. Pick out a four-bar phrase and see if the scale degrees used have been altered from the key signature at the start of the piece. If they have, this could indicate a form of minor scale.

GOALS

1 *Understand the construction of the natural minor scale.*
2 *Know the names and differences in the three forms of minor scale.*
3 *Find minor key signatures by using the circle of fifths.*
4 *Know the difference between parallel and relative minor.*

Answers

EXERCISE 10.2

E – natural
minor scale

D♯ raised for harmonic minor scale

E – melodic
minor scale

a) D – harmonic minor

b) C – melodic minor

EXERCISE 10.3

C minor = 3 flats	F minor = 4 flats	B minor = 2 sharps
G minor = 2 flats	B♭ minor = 5 flats	F♯ minor = 3 sharps

EXERCISE 10.4

a) A minor = no sharps or flats   B minor = 2 sharps
b) F minor = 4 flats   B♭ minor = 5 flats   C♯ minor = 4 sharps

TEST YOURSELF

1 Which series of notes produces the pattern for a natural minor scale?

2 To form a melodic minor scale from the natural form, what alterations are made?

3 How is a harmonic minor scale formed from the natural minor?

4 Write out the pattern using the letters T and S for a natural minor scale.

5 What is the name of the pitch raised to form a harmonic minor scale, starting on F?

6 Using the circle of fifths, what is the key signature for the key of C minor?

7 What would be altered to change the C minor scale in natural form to melodic form?

8 Are C major and A minor parallel key signatures?

9 How are E minor and G major related?

10 Which degrees of a major scale are altered to form a blues scale?

11

Compound time signatures

In order to participate in music, whether as a listener, player or singer, it is important to understand how to count in various time signatures. A melody is completely unrecognizable if the rhythm is incorrect.
So far in this book, you have learned about the time signatures of $\frac{2}{4}$, $\frac{3}{4}$ and $\frac{4}{4}$. These are referred to as simple time signatures. There is another set of signatures for compound time, the most common being $\frac{6}{8}$.

Counting $\frac{6}{8}$

In the time signature of $\frac{6}{8}$ there are six beats in each bar. The difference is that now the quaver (eighth note) gets the beat instead of the crotchet (quarter note). The first beat is strong, followed by two weak beats on 2 and 3. The fourth beat is medium strong, but not as strong as the first beat. Beats 5 and 6 are weak. Quavers (eighth notes) are grouped as follows:

In $\frac{6}{8}$, the two strong beats on 1 and 4 give an underlying feel of counting in two. In fact, if music written in $\frac{6}{8}$ is to be performed at a fast tempo, it is usually conducted in two, not six.

> ## Insight
>
> Some students find it difficult to understand the compound
> feel of ⁶⁄₈. A helpful way to learn this is to continually tap
> 123456 with one hand and with your other hand, tap the
> underlying 'one' on the first beat, and the 'two' on the fourth
> beat. Warning! It might take a bit of co-ordination practice!

When notating quavers in ⁶⁄₈ join them so that the division between
the third and fourth beats is clear.

Exercise 11.1 (Listening)

Music written in ⁶⁄₈ time has a lilting feel, like someone skipping.
Popular tunes which use ⁶⁄₈ include 'I saw three ships', 'For he's
a jolly good fellow' and 'Greensleeves'. Hum these tunes to
yourself and see if you are able to feel the lilting rhythm. Listen
to a demonstration of ⁶⁄₈ played on the keyboard. You should
be able to hear the six quavers (eighth notes) as well as the two
underlying strong beats on the first and fourth counts of each bar.

Exercise 11.2 (Written)

Complete the written exercises using ⁶⁄₈ by adding notes, stems or
rests as needed.

Add bar-lines to make the following into $\frac{6}{8}$.

a) $\frac{6}{8}$

b) $\frac{6}{8}$

c) $\frac{6}{8}$

Insight

After you have checked that your answers to Exercise 11.2 are correct, try clapping the rhythms. This provides yet more practice in learning the feeling of $\frac{6}{8}$.

Exercise 11.3 (Practical)

Practise clapping these $\frac{6}{8}$ rhythms. Remember to count two bars before you start clapping.

a) $\frac{6}{8}$

b) $\frac{6}{8}$

c) This one is written in two parts. Learn each part, then tap one part with your left hand while your right taps the other!

Exercise 11.4 (Practical)

For the final exercise using $\frac{6}{8}$, you will be playing along with the CD. Here is a short piece of music. While the tune is played, you are to clap the rhythm along to the music. Instructions will be given before you start.

(Contd)

Insight

Here is another way to practise Exercise 11.4. With your right
hand tap 123456 continually while your left hand taps the
rhythm of the tune. After you feel confident, turn the CD back
on and perform this new arrangement along with the music.

Other compound time signatures

Besides ⁶₈, the time signatures of ⁹₈ and ¹²₈ are occasionally found in
music.

In ⁹₈ time, there are nine quavers (eighth notes) to each bar, the
quaver still receiving one beat. There is an underlying feel of three.

For ¹²₈ time, there are 12 quavers (eighth notes) to each bar, the
quaver getting one beat. There is an underlying feeling of four.

⊚ Exercise 11.5 (Listening)

Listen to a demonstration of $\frac{9}{8}$ and $\frac{12}{8}$ time.

Insight

Listening to a demonstration is helpful, but you'll never be sure you're completely clear until you play the rhythms. Using the examples in Exercise 11.5, see how your get on. Chant the numbers 1 2 3 4 5 6 7 8 9 or 1 2 3 4 5 6 7 8 9 10 11 12 while tapping the underlying beats.

Comparing simple and compound time

The following table shows a comparison between simple and compound time signatures.

Simple duple	$\frac{2}{4}$ ♩ ♩ ‖ 1 2	Compound duple (underlying beat)	$\frac{6}{8}$ ♫♫ ♫♫ ‖ 1 2 3 4 5 6 1 2
Simple triple	$\frac{3}{4}$ ♩ ♩ ♩ ‖ 1 2 3	Compound triple	$\frac{9}{8}$ ♫♫ ♫♫ ♫♫ ‖ 1 2 3 4 5 6 7 8 9 1 2 3
Simple quadruple	$\frac{4}{4}$ ♩ ♩ ♩ ♩ ‖ 1 2 3 4	Compound quadruple	$\frac{12}{8}$ ♫♫ ♫♫ ♫♫ ♫♫ ‖ 1 2 3 4 5 6 7 8 9 10 11 12 1 2 3 4

Insight

Understanding the differences between simple time and compound time is vital if your counting is to be correct. I would suggest memorizing the chart above. If you do, this important information will always be available.

$\frac{5}{8}$ AND $\frac{7}{8}$

In the time signatures of $\frac{5}{8}$ and $\frac{7}{8}$, the accents can be arranged in different ways as shown here:

Exercise 11.6 (Practical)

Practise clapping the previous example, noticing the difference in feel when the accent is changed.

Exercise 11.7 (Practical – rhythm dictation)

The skeletons for three rhythms follow. Each will be played five times, with gaps left in between each playing for you to write down what you heard. Notice the time signature before starting each one.

a) $\frac{6}{8}$ | | | ‖

b) $\frac{9}{8}$ | | | ‖

c) $\frac{5}{8}$ | | | ‖

GOALS

1 *Know the meaning of the time signature of $\frac{6}{8}$.*
2 *Be able to write and perform $\frac{6}{8}$ rhythms correctly.*
3 *Understand the compound time signatures of $\frac{9}{8}$ and $\frac{12}{8}$ and their underlying feel.*

Answers

EXERCISE 11.2

a)

b)

c)

Bar-lines

a)

b)

c)

EXERCISE 11.7

a) $\frac{6}{8}$ ♫♫ ♩. | ♫♫ ♫♩ ⁊ | ♩. ♩. | ♫♫ ♩. ‖

b) $\frac{9}{8}$ ♫♫ ♩. ♫♫ | ♫♫ ♫♫ ♩. | ♩. ♫♫ ♩. | ♫♫ ♫♫ ♩. ‖

c) $\frac{5}{8}$ ♫ ♫♫ | ♩ ♫♫ | ♫ ⁊ ♫ | ♫ ♫♫ ‖

TEST YOURSELF

1 Is ⅝ a simple or compound time signature?

2 What is the underlying feel in ⅝?

3 How many beats are in a bar of ⅝, and what type of note gets the beat?

4 Which type of note gets one beat in ⅜?

5 What about ¹²⁄₈? Which type of note gets the beat?

6 Name a simple duple metre.

7 Name a simple quadruple metre.

8 Is ¾ a compound duple metre?

9 Give two ways ⅝ may be accented.

10 Now give two ways ⅞ may be accented.

12

Introducing chords

You have already learned how different rhythms and pitches are combined to form melodies. Music having only a single melody line with no accompaniment is called monophonic. This style was used by the ancient Greeks and in Gregorian chant, the music of the Roman Catholic church named after Pope Gregory I, dating from around 600 AD. Other examples of monophonic music include oriental music and folk songs. When accompaniment is added to a melody line, the music becomes fuller and richer. Using chords is one way of enhancing a melody.

Three or more notes sounded together make a chord. Two notes sounded together are considered an interval, not a chord. There is no limit to the number of notes in a chord and some instruments such as the piano or guitar can play more than one single pitch at one time. Chords are also formed when two or more musicians or singers sound different notes which blend together. The notes of one chord can also be spread throughout the many instruments of an entire symphony orchestra.

Major and minor triads

The simplest type of chord is the triad, consisting of three notes. (Think of a tricycle with three wheels or a triangle with three sides.) When the triad is in root position, the root is the lowest note in the chord, with the third and fifth written above it, arranged in intervals of a third. The two basic types of triads are major and minor. In the major, the interval between the root and third is a major third or four semitones. The interval between the third and fifth is a minor third or three semitones. In a minor triad, the intervals are reversed. The interval between the root and third is a minor third and the major third is now found between the third and fifth. Although there is only a slight difference in the construction between major and minor triads, their sounds are quite unique. In simple terms, a major triad sounds bright and cheerful while the minor is sad and mysterious (see below).

Examples of major and minor triads with intervals marked

C   D   G   C mi   D mi   G mi

🎵 Exercise 12.1 (Listening)

Study the examples of major and minor triads that follow. Notice how accidentals have been added to form the correct intervals. The triads are written in root position with the lowest note actually being the root note. Listen to the demonstration of the triads as they are played.

Examples of major triads

F   E   B♭   A   F

Examples of minor triads

A mi   F mi   G mi   C mi   B mi

Major and minor triads on the keyboard

C major triad   C minor triad

Write either a major or minor triad as indicated in root position, adding accidentals where needed.

D minor   E major   F minor   G major   B♭ major   E minor

Inversions

Triads are often used in an arrangement where the root note of the chord is not the lowest. The notes used in the triad stay the same, but they are arranged in a different order. These are called inversions of a triad.

The first example a) shows C and G major triads written in three different positions. When moving from the root position to the first inversion, the bottom note has been moved to the top and is an octave higher. The same is true when moving from the first inversion to the second inversion. The second example b) shows a C major chord moving to a G major chord. The movement is made much easier by using the first inversion of the G chord. Example c) shows a minor triad with inversions.

a)

C triad   G triad

b)

C   G   C   C   G   C
(first inversion)

c)

F minor

Exercise 12.3 (Written)

Practise writing inversions of the following triads:

E minor

A major

F major

EXERCISE

Augmented and diminished triads

Major and minor triads can be altered to become augmented and diminished. Augmenting a chord creates more space between the intervals of the third and fifth in root position. Augmented triads are easily made by starting with a major triad in root position and raising the fifth one semitone. A diminished triad is easily made from a minor triad in root position by lowering the fifth one semitone. This reduces the space between the third and fifth (see below).

Examples of augmented and diminished triads

major   aug.   minor   dim.

Insight

Remember that an augmented triad is easily made from a major triad, and a diminished from a minor triad. If you want to make a major triad diminished, it first must be made minor, then diminished. If you want to make a minor triad augmented, first make it major, then augmented.

Keyboard examples showing augmented and diminished triads

C augmented   C diminished

 Exercise 12.4 (Listening)

Listen to the demonstration about constructing augmented and diminished triads. Their sound will be compared with that of major and minor triads.

EXERCISE

Exercise 12.5 (Written)

Change the following major triads to augmented by adding the necessary accidentals:

Make diminished triads out of the following minor triads, adding accidentals where needed:

> ### Insight
>
> It takes lots of practice to fully understand the construction of augmented and diminished triads. Why not transpose line a) in Exercise 12.5 to bass clef and line b) to treble clef? After you have done this, repeat the initial exercise. This will also provide further practice in transposition!

Chord symbols

In popular music especially, a type of abbreviation is used to indicate the accompaniment chords. For a major chord, just the letter-name appears. For minor, a small m is placed after the letter-name. Aug. or + denotes augmented chords and dim. or ○ is used for diminished. Chord symbols are most commonly written above the melody line and are used in guitar and keyboard music. The complete chord is not written out in full. The musician is expected to know how to construct the given chords from the symbols.

Example of chord symbols written above the staff and located at the beginning of each bar

Insight

Knowing how to construct a chord from a chord symbol is a necessary skill, especially if you are planning to study popular music. See if you can find some sheet music of popular songs, then try to figure out what the basic chord symbols mean. At first, it's best to stick to the straightforward symbols like major and minor.

 Exercise 12.6 (Practical)

Identify each type of chord you hear as either major, minor, augmented or diminished. Write your answers in the blank spaces, using chord symbols.

_____ _____ _____ _____ _____ _____ _____

_____ _____ _____ _____ _____ _____ _____

_____

Added note chords

THE SEVENTH CHORD

Extra notes are often added to the basic triad to give interest and colour. The seventh above the root note is the most common and the interval of a minor seventh is mostly used. For chord symbols, a small 7 is added following the letter-name. Any type of triad, whether major, minor, augmented or diminished, can have an added seventh.

Examples of seventh chords written in root position with added chord symbols

The seventh chord has three inversions instead of two because there are now four notes in the chord, not three.

Inversions of the seventh chord

The idea of adding notes to a triad may be carried further to form chords containing a ninth, eleventh and thirteenth above the root note. Although these more elaborate chords add interest, they also create a weaker key feeling because of the added notes which do not belong to the basic triad. Chords with added notes are found in jazz and also in impressionistic music by composers of the Romantic era (1820–1900) such as Debussy.

Examples of added note chords

Insight

If you are finding added note chords confusing, narrow it down at first to just finding a root note, and counting up from it. This will help in establishing the distance between the root and the added note, eliminating all of the other pitches in between.

Exercise 12.7 (Listening)

Listen to a demonstration of different chords with added notes.

Notation of chords

When writing chords out in full on one staff, the stem joins all the notes together. Addition of the stem follows the rule of going upwards if the majority of the note heads are below the third line or downwards if the note heads are above the third line. Chords written this way are seen in music for piano. If separate parts are written on the same staff, the stems are written in different directions to separate each part clearly. This is common in vocal music.

Answers

EXERCISE 12.2

D minor   E major   F minor   G major   B♭ major   E minor

EXERCISE 12.3

E minor

A major

F major

EXERCISE 12.5

Aug.   Dim.

EXERCISE 12.6
M, m, M, M, +, ○, M, m, +, ○, m, +, +. M.

TEST YOURSELF

1 Define a chord.

2 What is a triad?

3 Name two basic types of triad.

4 If a triad is arranged so the root note is at the bottom, with
   the third and fifth written above, in which position is the
   triad?

5 How is the construction of a minor triad different from a
   major?

6 If the notes of a triad are arranged so the root is not on the
   bottom, what is it called?

7 In an inversion, do the pitches change?

8 What is the term for a major chord made larger?

9 Define a chord symbol.

10 Describe an added note chord.

13

Harmony

In the previous chapter, you learned about the structure of individual chords. This chapter goes further in explaining the relationships between chords within a scale and also covers some of the basics of counterpoint. In music where the melody is supported by chords, the texture is referred to as harmonic, harmony being the study of chords. Another approach to adding texture is by writing melodies against each other. This is called counterpoint and the music is referred to as contrapuntal or polyphonic.

Chord names and functions

Triads can be built on each degree of a scale. The mode, either major or minor, does not matter. Roman numerals are used to identify each chord. They also have names which show their function and placement within the scale.

Example of triads built on the scale of C

I II III IV V VI VII

I *Tonic – the keynote. The name of the scale is based on this.*
II *Supertonic – the note directly above the tonic.*

III *Mediant – located halfway between the tonic and dominant.*

IV *Subdominant – has the same relationship to the upper tonic note as the dominant has from the starting tonic, that of a fifth.*

V *Dominant – next in importance to the tonic in establishing key feeling.*

VI *Mediant – midway between the tonic and subdominant.*

VII *Leading note – a chord with the strong feeling of leading to the tonic.*

The most important chords in establishing the key feeling in any scale are the primary triads of I, IV and V. The other triads are referred to as secondary and function as substitutes for the primary triads to add interest and colour to music.

 Exercise 13.1 (Listening)

Listen to the demonstration of each of the triads of a scale played on the CD.

> **Insight**
>
> It is important to get to know the sounds of the progessions between different chords. Since the I, IV and V are the most important in defining the key feeling, a good starting place is to hum or sing the upward movement of the intervals of the roots in that progession. I up to IV is a perfect fourth and IV up to V is a major second. Lots of popular and folk songs are based on these three chords.

Cadences

Cadences are found at the end of a musical phrase and provide a pause in the music. The progression of chords leading to the cadence defines the strength of the pause, as described in the following. The examples are written for four separate parts called voices. This is chorale style and will be explained in more detail later in this chapter.

1 *The cadence using V moving to I is called a perfect or authentic cadence and has a final feeling about it. Usually a IV chord precedes the V chord, making the chord progression of IV, V, I.*

Example of a perfect or authentic cadence in D major

2 *The plagal cadence is a chord progression of IV to I. It is also known as the 'Amen' cadence.*

Example of a plagal cadence in C major

3 *An interrupted or deceptive cadence occurs when the expected tonic chord is replaced by another chord, sometimes the VI. It creates an element of surprise because the expected ending did not happen.*

Example of an interrupted or deceptive cadence in F major

IV   V   VI

4 *The imperfect or half cadence is a chord progression of I to V.*

Example of an imperfect or half cadence in G major

I   V

EXERCISE

Exercise 13.2 (Listening and practical)

Listen to the musical examples as the cadences are played on the CD. A series of cadences will then be played for you to identify. Jot down your answers as you listen.

Chorale style

Writing chords in four voice parts, also called the chorale style, is the beginning point for the study of harmony. When writing a triad for four voices, one note of the chord will need to be used twice. Where possible, the root is the best note to double. Before actually starting to write in chorale style, it is helpful first to practise writing chords with just the root note in the bass and the rest of the chord in root position in the treble clef.

Write the following chords with the root note in the bass and the rest of the chord in treble clef, root position. An example has been done for you.

FOUR VOICES SPLIT EQUALLY

The four voices used in basic chorale style are based on the human voices of soprano, alto, tenor and bass. Their ranges are shown in the example.

Ranges of the human voice

| Soprano | Alto | Tenor | Bass |

....
Insight
 The information in Figure 13.7 shows the extremes of the various voice ranges. If you look through any vocal music, you will see that most melodies don't make use of an entire range.
....

The rule of doubling the root note still applies, but the voices are now split equally between the treble and bass clefs, the soprano and alto in the treble clef, and tenor and bass voices in the bass clef. The following example shows a chord progression of I, IV, V, I in the key of G major. Although inversions may be used, the example uses all the chords in root position. When inversions are used, small numbers called figured bass (see below) may be written below the Roman numerals to identify the inversions. Notice the directions of the stems in chorale style. The soprano and tenor stems go up while the alto and bass go down. This is done to separate the parts clearly and make reading easier. Basic rules of four-part writing state that there should not be more than an octave between soprano and alto or between the alto and tenor. Notes common to two consecutive chords should be held over and the leading note must rise to the tonic note to resolve the tension created.

Example of four-part writing

Exercise 13.4 (Listening)

Listen to a demonstration of the last example.

Figured bass

Understanding figured bass is an involved process, but the example that follows gives a very general idea of how these numbers are used. As previously mentioned, small numbers called figured bass define the inversions of chords used. Look at the example of a C major chord in first inversion. Assuming that the C chord is the I chord in the key, the figured bass would be written I_3^6. This means that there is a note the interval of a sixth written somewhere above the bass note. This would be the note C. The G is the note an interval of a third above the bottom note, E. (Note that the G octave is not counted or the interval would be compound, that of a tenth.)

Example of figured bass

Counterpoint

Counterpoint is a way of adding texture to music by writing melodies against other melodies. Each part is called a voice. Many people feel that counterpoint is difficult to understand with its various melodic lines competing against one another. However, imitation is important to counterpoint and anyone who has ever participated in singing a simple tune as a round with the melody entering at several points has helped create counterpoint!

Instead of a long flowing melody, short, brief melodic figures called motifs are used in counterpoint. One form commonly used in writing counterpoint is the fugue. It is usually in three or four voices and has a subject that enters in various ways throughout the voices to form an interesting and intricate texture.

Example of simple counterpoint written for two voices

Modulation

When you studied scales, the emphasis was on establishing a feeling of being in a certain key or tonal centre. This is very important if a piece of music is going to hold together. In spite of this, a composition of any length will become uninteresting if it continually uses just the harmonies available in one key centre. A change of key centre or mode provides variety and a feeling that the piece has moved away from its beginning point. Changing the key centre during a composition is called modulation. It usually occurs at the end of a phrase or section of a larger work, but should only be used after the initial key centre has been firmly established. If modulation occurs too soon, i.e. before the original key is established, the listener may experience some confusion as to key feeling.

There are several ways to change keys within a piece and this depends somewhat on the style of the music. Some modulations are quite abrupt and make the change very noticeable, yet others are much more subtle. Because the many different methods used to change key are beyond the scope of this book, only the most common will be introduced.

PIVOT CHORD

A frequently used device for modulation is called the 'pivot chord'. The transition involves using a chord both common and closely related to both the original key and the new key.

Exercise 13.5 (Listening)

Study the 'Jig' that follows. You will see that it is in two sections, each one repeated. The piece begins in the key of F but moves away from it, the first section ending in C. This is confirmed by the B♭ being cancelled by the natural sign, temporarily establishing the key of C major. The second section begins in C major and works its way back to end in F major. The relationship between the keys of F major and C is a fifth. Now listen to 'Jig' played on the CD, noting the change in key in the first section.

'Jig'

Another type of modulation is the change between relative major and minor keys. Listen to the next example, which changes between the relative keys of A minor and C major.

Use of a chromatic move is much more abrupt than changing to a related key. The example that follows shows a chromatic change by moving from C major to C♯ major. The music is transposed up one semitone. This type of modulation is often used in popular songs at the beginning of a verse to show a movement forward in time. Listen to the example on the CD.

When listening to the two examples in Exercises 13.6 and
13.7, it might become necessary to do a bit of review work.
Exercise 13.6 won't make sense unless you are clear about
relative and parallel key signatures. For Exercise 13.7, you
must be sure about semitones or half tones and whole tones.
If anything is confusing, be sure to go back and sort it out
before moving on.

GOALS

1 *Know the names and functions of the chords built on
   each degree of a scale.*
2 *Understand and recognize cadences.*
3 *Know the basics of writing chords in four-part
   chorale style.*
4 *Define 'counterpoint'.*
5 *Understand the basic kinds of modulation.*

Answers

EXERCISE 13.2
Plagal, half or imperfect, deceptive or interrupted, authentic or
perfect, half or imperfect, authentic or perfect, plagal.

EXERCISE 13.3

C   G mi   A   F   E mi   B♭

TEST YOURSELF

1 When a melody is supported by chords, what is the texture called?

2 Which are the three most important chords in establishing the key feeling?

3 Give another name for the 'Amen' cadence.

4 Which is the best note to double in chorale-style writing for four parts?

5 To which note must the leading note resolve in chorale-style writing?

6 Write the figured bass used to show a chord in first inversion.

7 Is a fugue a style of harmonic writing?

8 Define a motif.

9 In modulation, what is a pivot chord?

10 Is changing from a relative major key to its relative minor a way of modulating?

14

Adding accompaniment to a melody

Especially in popular and folk music, you may come across a written melody having no written accompaniment or chord symbols indicated. A complete study of adding chords and chord progressions is lengthy and beyond the scope of this book. However, this chapter attempts to give an introduction to the basic steps involved in adding a simple chord accompaniment to a given melody by using chord symbols.

Finding the most suitable chords

'Folk tune'

'Folk tune' is an easy melody written in the key of C. It needs some chord symbols added as accompaniment. The best way to start is by first writing out a C major scale in treble clef, then building a triad above each scale degree, and marking each chord as major or minor. (Note that the VII chord is diminished and should not be used in this exercise.) It is also helpful to make a chart showing the note names found in each of the triads in the key of C. Remember that the three most important chords in any key are I, IV and V.

Insight

Deciding on the best chords when adding accompaniment to a given melody is not an easy task, especially in the learning stages. See if you can find some easy tunes similar to 'Folk tune', also written in the key of C major. After you have added chords to 'Folk tune', you will gain more practice by doing the same to your tunes.

Triads in the key of C

I	II	III	IV	V	VI	VII	VIII
C	D mi	E mi	F	G	A mi	B dim.	C

Note names found in each triad

I (C) = C E G   II (D) = D F A   III (E) = E G B   IV (F) = F A C
V (G) = G B D   VI (A) = A C E   VII (B) = B D F

Insight

Although the types of triad (major, minor or diminished) are included in Figure 14.2, only the names of the notes found in each chord are written in the box above. It would be helpful for you to indicate which ones are minor or diminished, and also circle the most important chords of I, IV and V. These are the chords you want to use most!

When adding chords for accompaniment, keep the process as simple as possible, only changing chords when necessary, usually once or twice per bar. Most simple music begins and ends with the tonic or keynote chord, C in this case. Let's work out an accompaniment for 'Folk tune'.

The first bar contains two pitches, C and G. Because the tune is in the key of C and both C and G are present in a C major triad, adding a C major chord would be the logical choice for that entire bar. I have written the chord symbol for C above the melody line at the beginning of bar one. The second bar uses only one pitch, F. Because the F major chord is the IV chord, an important chord in the key of C, I have decided to use it, not the D or B chords which are secondary in importance. The third bar is more complicated; now you *are* spoiled for choice! The second note, E, is on a weak beat and serves as a link between the F and D in the melody, so does not affect the choice of chord. Study the chart of note names in each triad: the choices available are either the D minor or F triad. F has already been used throughout the previous bar, so a change would be welcome. The final two notes of the third bar, D and G, would suggest a G major chord. I would use two chords in that bar, the D minor for the first two beats followed by the G major. The fourth bar is the end of the phrase and needs a cadence. I have again used two chords in that bar, C major and G major, making an imperfect or half cadence of I to V. The beginning of the next phrase has notes in the melody that outline a C major triad – C, E, G – so C is the obvious choice. In the sixth bar, the important notes are the F and A and suggest either the F chord or the D minor. I think the F chord would be best, followed by the D minor and G in the next bar. This follows the same scheme as in the first phrase.

The second example of 'Folk tune' shows the most logical chord symbols written above the melody line. The chords in brackets are some of the alternatives.

 Exercise 14.1 (Listening)

Turn on the CD and listen to 'Folk tune' with different chords added as accompaniments. Decide for yourself which ones sound best!

(Contd)

EXERCISE

The tune is in the key of C major, so beginning and ending on any chord other than C will not establish the key feeling. Also, bar four is an imperfect or half cadence, so using the chord of G best defines this.

'Folk tune'

Exercise 14.2 (Written)

The melody of a well-known tune is written in this exercise in the key of D major. Following the same process as earlier for 'Folk tune', decide on a simple accompaniment and write the chord symbols above the melody line. Be sure to make a chart showing the names of the notes present in each chord.

I   II   III   IV   V   VI   VII   VIII

Insight

After you have written out your triads for the key of D major, change the key signature to one flat, and do the same for D minor. Notice that the important triads of I, IV and V are now minor, not major.

'The fox'

Transposing melody and accompaniment

A lot of music is written in a key which is difficult to sing or play. If this is the case, you will need to transpose both the melody and accompaniment up or down to a more comfortable key. This process is similar to transposing an octave, which you have previously done. It might be helpful to have a diagram of the keyboard available for reference.

Let's look again at 'Folk tune' written in the key of C. You have decided that it is too low and want to transpose it up to G major. The note G is the interval of a perfect fifth, seven semitones above C. The first step is to transpose all the notes in the melody line up a perfect fifth. The rhythm stays the same, but remember to add the key signature of the new key. Finally, transpose the chord symbols up the interval of a perfect fifth. The example that follows shows 'Folk tune' transposed to the key of G.

'Folk tune'

Exercise 14.3 (Written and listening)

Transpose the melody of 'The fox' down one whole tone from D major to the key of C, then add the appropriate chord symbols. After you have finished, turn on the CD and listen to 'The fox' played in both its original key and new key.

'The fox'

Writing an accompaniment

In the previous exercises, the accompaniments were notated as chord symbols, a common method suitable for guitar. The performer usually improvises a suitable accompaniment, using the chord symbols as a guide. Chords functioning as accompaniment may also be written in full music notation. The new example shows 'Folk tune' (in C) with the accompaniment written in block chords, all in root position. This is a common way to add simple accompaniment to piano or keyboard music. The melody is in the treble clef and played with the right hand. The chords are written in the bass clef and played with the left hand.

Part of 'Folk tune' with block chords

🎵 Exercise 14.4 (Written)

The first part of the melody for 'The fox' is written here in the treble clef. Add block chords in root position in the bass clef.

'The fox'

🎵 Exercise 14.5 (Listening)

Listen to 'Folk tune' and 'The fox' played with block chord accompaniment.

Inversions of chords are often used to make the movements between chords easier. Study the first part of 'Folk tune' with inversions used in the accompaniment. Notice how much easier it is to move between chords.

(Contd)

C Root position　　F 2nd inversion　　D mi Root position　G 2nd inversion　C Root position　G 1st inversion

> ## Insight
>
> When learning to add chord accompaniments, it is easier to first use block chords. However, this sort of accompaniment will require lots of jumping about with the left hand! Remember that it is best to change the root position triads to an inversion for a smoother accompaniment.

Exercise 14.6 (Listening)

Besides block chords, there are different ways in which chords can be arranged into interesting patterns. Listen to a demonstration of four examples of accompaniments played on the piano.

GOALS

1. *Be able to add basic chords to a simple melody line by using chord symbols.*
2. *Know how to convert chord symbols into block chords.*
3. *Transpose melodies and chords to other keys.*

TEST YOURSELF

1 *What is a helpful thing to do when preparing to add a chord accompaniment?*

2 *Which are the three most important chords in establishing the key feeling?*

3 *In the key of C major, is the VI chord major or minor?*

4 *When adding an accompaniment, how often should the chords change?*

5 *In the first bar of a tune written in C major, why is a C chord a better choice than an A minor chord?*

6 *What about ending the same piece on the A minor chord?*

7 *Why would you need to transpose a tune?*

8 *When transposing a melody, does the accompaniment also need to be transposed?*

9 *How is a melody and accompaniment written for piano?*

10 *Why are inversions of chords sometimes used in the accompaniment?*

15

Musical form

You have seen throughout the book how different elements are combined to make music. However, rhythm, pitch and melody need to be further organized by a basic plan called musical form. The form of a composition functions like a roadmap. This chapter explores some of the basic points about musical forms.

Repetition

Using repetition is one way to help hold a work together. There are special signs used to show when sections of a composition are to be performed more than once. The use of signs saves space and time by removing the need for the music to be written out again.

THE REPEAT SIGN

One of the most common signs used is called the repeat sign and is written as double lines with two dots placed to the left. When reaching a repeat sign, look for a similar sign with dots on the right and repeat the music contained between the two signs. If there is no matching sign, then return to the beginning of the piece and repeat from there. Once the repeated section has been performed, continue on with the new music after the repeat sign.

Follow the musical example as it is played, observing the repeats.

FIRST AND SECOND TIME BARS

This type of repeat is similar to the repeat sign. The difference is that on the first performance, a bar marked with a bracket and the number 1, called the first time bar, is used. After the second performance, the first time bar is replaced by a different bar called the second time bar. It is marked with a bracket and number 2. Skip over the first time bar and replace it with the second time bar. Do not play the first time bar as well or you will have too many bars in your piece!

Example showing first and second time bars

Insight

Although repeat signs are used to save space, they can be difficult to follow, especially when the music has several repetitions. Always look through the piece, making sure you know your way around BEFORE trying to play it. It's one less thing to have to think about. Draw little reminders if necessary.

REPEATED BARS

Sometimes, just one bar or even part of a bar is to be repeated several times. A stroke is used to represent each time the bar or section of the bar is to be repeated. To indicate several bars of silence, a long rest sign with the number of bars is used. This is commonly found in music for ensembles.

Examples of repeated bars

DC AL FINE

The appearance of the words **DC al fine** instructs the performer to return to the beginning of the work and play until reaching the word 'fine' (finish). The da capo aria is a song form used extensively in opera and provides an opportunity for a soloist to show off his or her vocal capabilities. On the repeat performance, the original material is decorated and embellished, adding to the emotional impact of the aria.

The abbreviation DS means **dal segno**. Instead of returning to the beginning of a work, the performer repeats from where the 'sign' appears (see example below).

Introduction and coda

Many musical works, whether short songs or larger compositions, have an introduction at the beginning. It may range from a few bars to an entire opening section. A coda is found at the end of a work and contains extra bars to give the work a finished feeling. In larger works, the coda may serve as a deception, leading on again when the listener expected the music to end.

Form represented by letters

The plan or design of different music is often diagrammed by using letter-names. Some of the most common forms represented by letters are described in the following sections. These can be found in individual pieces such as songs or can be part of a much larger work.

STROPHIC – A A A A A

Music is strophic if all the verses or stanzas are set to the same music. This form is used extensively in hymns and folk tunes. The 'A' represents the use of the same music repeated for every verse although the words change. Sometimes a refrain is used in a strophic song. In this form, there is still a series of verses using the same music. A refrain is a line of lyrics repeated at the end of each verse. The last line of each verse, therefore, uses the same words although the words in the rest of each verse change. An example of a song using a refrain is 'Blowin' in the wind'.

THEME AND VARIATIONS – A´ A´´ A´´´ A´´´´

In a work of theme and variations, the original melody, the theme, is first presented, usually in a simple style. It is then repeated, but varied in a different way. A 'prime sign' is added after the letter 'A' for each different variation of the theme.

BINARY (TWO-PART) FORM – A B

A piece written in binary form contains two different sections of music. A common example would be a song having an alternating verse and chorus. This is a form popular for songs because it provides forward movement of the story through each verse alternating with repetition of an important thought restated in the chorus. The music for the verse and music for the chorus are different, the verse being 'A' and the chorus 'B'. The words of each verse change, but the words for the chorus stay the same or nearly the same each time it is repeated.

TERNARY (THREE-PART) FORM – A B A

This is music consisting of three sections. The first and third are the same, with the middle section contrasting.

RONDO – A B A C A D A E

The main characteristic of a rondo is the repetition of the original material, labelled as 'A', alternating with new material. Following each repeat of 'A', new and unrelated music is introduced. It is the constant return of the original music that holds a rondo together.

Insight

The information above is fine as far as it goes. However, it is always better to see and hear music when working out its form. You can do this by either studying the written score or listening. By labelling the different sections as you go along, the form will eventually become clear.

SONATA OR FIRST MOVEMENT FORM

This form is frequently used for individual sections or pieces (movements) of a large work. It has three main sections, each having a special function. The exposition, beginning in the tonic key, presents the main musical material of the movement. The development section modulates through various keys and builds on the material from the exposition. Finally, the recapitulation more or less repeats the exposition, bringing the work to an ending, back in the tonic key:

| Intro (optional) | Exposition | Development section | Recapitulation | Coda (optional) |

COMPOSITE FORMS

These are large works having more than one movement, the symphony being an example. It often contains the following four movements:

1 *Fast, usually in sonata form.*
2 *Slow, occasionally using theme and variation form.*
3 *Minuet or other dance.*
4 *Fast, using rondo or sonata form.*

Other composite forms include the concerto – a work for solo instrument and orchestra; sonata – for a solo instrument such as piano; suite – a group of pieces sometimes related by being in the same key.

Insight

The sonata form is used extensively in music written during the Classical era, 1750–1820. You would be helped in understanding the form by listening to either a piano sonata or symphony composed by Mozart.

Words and music

Most of this book has dealt with the various aspects of music on its own, although through the ages, a lot of music has been combined with words. This includes sacred, secular, serious and light. In ancient Greece, music was treated as secondary and largely used to enhance the performance of the dramas. Only a few fragments of Greek music survive. These are three hymns and a drinking song!

After about 1600, opera began to develop and there was renewed controversy as to whether the words or the music were the more important element. Personally, I doubt the question can really be answered and this book is not the place for such a debate. The rest of this chapter will briefly explore how words combined with the form of a musical work help in telling stories through songs.

WHAT IS A SONG?

A song is actually a story written in rhyme. The words (lyrics) are set to a single line of melody. Accompaniment is also added to enhance the meaning of the words. The story told by the song can be fact or fiction, but must have a beginning, middle and end. It also must make a point! Just as in any story, there is a main character and maybe some minor ones, too.

Exercise 15.2 (Practical)

Study the lyrics and form of the song 'Love triangle'. This title suggests a situation that is perhaps common to many. A triangle is also a geometric shape and the chorus uses other shapes to help show the feelings of the singer. Try to imagine how you would feel if you were trapped in a corner of a triangle. You would probably be bent and feel small, unable to stand proud and tall. Think also how you would feel if you loved and trusted someone, then suddenly realized that person had lied about nearly everything. Your mind would probably be going round in circles. Although the singer feels hurt and confused, she is determined to find the strength to get free. She is 'boxed in' but fighting … like in a boxing ring. The form of the song is outlined in the lyrics.

'Love triangle'

Verse 1
A   I thought you really loved me, thought that you'd be true.
Couldn't believe I'd found a love as wonderful as you.
I thought about you all the time, and how our future'd be,
but I guess I never stopped to think that you would lie
    to me.

B   Chorus 1
I'm trapped in the corner of a love triangle, all because
    of you.
My head's spinning 'round in circles, don't know what
    to do.
I'm feeling all boxed in but fighting to get free.
I'm trapped in the corner of a love triangle 'cause you lied
    to me.

A   Verse 2
I knew that you were busy, believed you worked late.
Knew you needed someone patient, someone who
    would wait.
I believed your every word, you were my whole life,
but I found it hard believing that you have a wife! Now I'm.

B   Chorus 2
Trapped in the corner of a love triangle, all because
    of you.
My head's spinning 'round in circles, don't know what
    to do.
I'm feeling all boxed in but fighting to get free.
I'm trapped in the corner of a love triangle, you and her
    and me.

(Contd)

C   Bridge

Shame ... shame on you ...you can't have your cake and
   eat it too.

Shame ... shame on you ... you can only serve one love,
   not two.

B   Final chorus – as Chorus 1

> **Insight**
>
> When someone just listens to a song without really taking
> in its meaning, lots can be missed. It is important to get into
> the habit of not only listening to the lyrics of a song, but also
> searching for the story or meaning behind them.

GOALS

1 *Understand repeat signs.*
2 *Know how to represent the form of a musical work by using letters.*
3 *Understand the importance of words and musical form in creating songs.*

TEST YOURSELF

1 What is similar to a roadmap of a musical composition?

2 Give the description of a repeat sign.

3 When using first and second time bars, is the first time bar also repeated on the second playing?

4 'DC al fine' instructs a performer to do what?

5 How would binary form be represented in letters?

6 Which letters would represent a rondo?

7 What are the individual sections of a large work called?

8 Name the three main sections in sonata form.

9 A typical fourth movement of a symphony uses which tempo?

10 What are the words of a song called?

16

Tone colour and interpretation

Have you ever wondered why the same piece of music performed
by two different singers sounds so different even though the song
is arranged in exactly the same way? And why does a pitch played
on a trumpet have a different quality about it from the same pitch
played on a flute? The answer to these questions is the individual
tone colour or timbre of each voice or instrument. The same pitch
played on two different instruments sounds different because of the
construction of the instrument. This also affects instruments of the
same type. A cheap upright piano does not have the same quality in
sound as an expensive Steinway concert grand!

Different tone colours

The oldest and most natural instrument used in making music
is the human voice. It is the individual quality of each singing
voice that adds to the success of a performance. The way a voice
expresses emotion and conveys it to the audience makes some
performers extremely popular. Voices are also joined together in
choirs. A mixed choir using both male and female voices is divided
into four voice parts: soprano, alto, tenor and bass. The sound
produced by a mixed choir is entirely different from a purely male
voice choir or a choir consisting of only women's voices. Children's
voices produce yet another different tone colour from adult voices.

The range of tone colours made possible by using different
combinations of musical instruments is impossible to explain in

words. The modern symphony orchestra, for example, is arranged in sections of strings, woodwinds, brasses and percussion. The different tone qualities of individual instruments and combinations are easiest explained and learned by both listening to music and perhaps studying musical scores to see how the instruments are arranged.

Exercise 16.1 (Listening)

Listen to a demonstration of different tone colours.

Insight

I find it interesting to pick a piece of music and listen to different ways it has been performed. Sometimes a song is played as an instrumental, giving it a completely new feel without the lyrics. Even if it is sung by two different singers, it will sound very individual.

Arrangement and orchestration

An arrangement involves adapting music for voices or instruments different from the original. Orchestration is the process of arranging or scoring music for a symphony orchestra. The following table lists the instruments by section and in the standard order they are written on an orchestral score. Typical numbers of wind and brass instruments are shown, but not the actual number of each stringed instrument. If an instrument is not included anywhere in the composition, it will not be listed on the first page. In the rest of the score, each page only includes the instruments actually playing at that time.

Picc	𝄞	Piccolo
2 Fl	𝄞	Flutes
2 Ob	𝄞	Oboes

(Contd)

Eng Hrn	𝄞	Cor anglais or English horn	*Woodwinds*
2 Clar	𝄞	Clarinets	
2 Bsns	𝄢	Bassoons	
C Bsn	𝄢	Contrabassoon	
4 Hrns	𝄞	Horns	
2 Tpts	𝄞	Trumpets	
2 Trbs	𝄡 tenor clef	Trombones	*Brass*
Tuba	𝄢		
Timp	F$\sharp$, C, G	3 timpani, each tuned to a different pitch	*Percussion*
I Vl	𝄞	First violins	
II	𝄞	Second violins	
Vla	𝄡 alto clef	Violas	*Strings*
VC	𝄢	Cello	
DB	𝄢	Double bass	

The conductor

Many people question the need for a conductor. After all, he or she just seems to stand and wave a baton. In reality, a conductor has responsibilities including selecting the music, leading the rehearsals and deciding how the music is to be interpreted. Even though each player has a written part, the orchestra needs someone to stop and start everyone together, give cues and lead the changes in loudness and speed. A conductor usually leads with a baton in the right hand and uses the left to indicate the expression. In vocal music, the conductor uses both hands and does not usually use a baton.

CONDUCTING DIFFERENT TIME SIGNATURES

There are various patterns used to conduct both vocal and instrumental music. Some of the most common are found below, with arrows showing the direction the conductor follows. Practise following the patterns. When the arrow points downwards, that is the downbeat. An arrow pointing upwards is the upbeat.

🎵 Exercise 16.2 (Practical)

Turn on the CD and practise conducting the music provided.

Insight

You will gain further practice in conducting by listening to any type of music with a clear beat. First, identify the time signature. If the work is in a metre you don't recognize, leave that one and find another piece that is clearer. After being sure about the time signature, start conducting! This is valuable experience in developing your rhythmic feel.

Signs used to interpret music

You have seen how the way music is performed depends a lot on the artist, the arrangement, interpretation and personal taste. The composer does, however, usually give some indications by using certain signs for the desired speed, dynamics and overall feeling.

TEMPO

The speed of the music or tempo was touched on in Chapter 1. The terms used, mainly English and Italian, only suggest how fast the music is meant to be. Many composers now use their native language, with German and French becoming more common.

The following list contains some of the terms used for indicating tempo. They are arranged from slow to fast, many of them meaning more or less the same thing. (A more complete list of Italian terms is located at the back of this book.)

Largo	= slow, stately
Lento	= slow
Grave	= slow and solemn
Larghetto	= slightly faster than largo
Adagio	= slow, but not as slow as largo
Moderato	= moderate speed
Andante	= moderate, walking pace
Allegretto	= a little slower than allegro
Allegro	= quick, cheerful
Presto	= very fast, faster than allegro

When an accurate speed is desired by the composer, a metronome marking may be found at the beginning of the composition. The metronome is an instrument that clicks at a set rate. A metronome marking looks like this: M.M. $\quad \boldsymbol{\downarrow}$ = 110. This means that in one minute, 110 crotchets beats will be counted.

Composers may not give a tempo indication, but instead use descriptive words to define the feeling of a work. Examples include:

Dolce = sweetly
Grazioso = gracefully
Amoroso = lovingly
Giocoso = playfully

Titles such as minuet, lullaby or blues also give a performer clues about the style of a composition. In such cases, however, it is up to the performer to know the characteristics of that style of music in order to perform it properly.

Insight

It would be helpful for you to look through some printed music to see how the tempo is indicated. Eventually, you will need to learn the Italian terms so you'll know how fast or slow to play a piece. Learning a few terms at a time is the easiest way.

CHANGES IN SPEED

Music does not always stay at the same speed throughout and changes add variety and sometimes drama. There are various signs and musical terms used to indicate changes of tempo. A few of the most common are:

Accelerando *(accel.)* = gradually increasing speed (think of pressing the accelerator in a car!)
Rallentando *(rall.)* = getting gradually slower
Ritenuto *(rit.)* = getting slower
A tempo = go back to the original speed

⌒ = pause. Known as the fermata sign, if written over an individual note it indicates that it is to be held longer than normal. It is up to the performer to decide on the length the note is held. In group playing, the conductor would direct the hold.

DYNAMICS

Most music is performed using different levels of loudness and softness, referred to as dynamics. Words or signs are written below the staff at the beginning of the piece, with new instructions given throughout. Some of the most common signs and abbreviations for dynamics are as follows:

Piano (p)	= soft
Pianissimo (pp)	= very soft
Mezzo piano (mp)	= medium soft
Forte (f)	= loud
Fortissimo (ff)	= very loud
Mezzo forte (mf)	= medium loud
Sforzando (sfz)	= suddenly loud
Crescendo (cresc.)	= gradually becoming louder
Decrescendo/diminuendo (dim.)	= gradually becoming softer.

Signs for crescendo and diminuendo are $\prec$ and $\succ$.

ARTICULATION

Articulation is the way an individual note is performed. Some of the signs used are as follows:

Accent		note played with a strong stress
Staccato		a dot placed over or under the head of note indicating it should be played as short as possible
Pedal	ped.	shows when the sustaining or right pedal on the piano should be pressed and released
Slur		a curved line written above or below the heads of a series of notes indicating that these notes should be played smoothly; found in vocal music; also used to give bowing instructions for stringed instruments

GOALS

1 *Understand about tone colour or timbre.*
2 *Know the difference between an arrangement and orchestration.*
3 *Be able to conduct music in basic time signatures.*
4 *Know some of the words and signs that are used in interpreting music (speed, articulation, dynamics).*

TEST YOURSELF

1 Why does a pitch played on a flute have a different quality from the same pitch played on a trombone?

2 What is scoring music for a symphony orchestra called?

3 On a full orchestral score, is the exact number of string players shown?

4 After the first page of a score, do all of the instruments continue to be shown on each page?

5 When leading an orchestra, which hand does the conductor use to indicate expression?

6 Does the word largo refer to tempo or dynamics?

7 Describe a metronome.

8 Give the definition of the phrase 'A tempo'.

9 What are dynamics?

10 Define articulation.

17

....

Ornaments and non-harmonic notes

Throughout the ages, most music has used embellishment and ornamentation to some degree. Many students, however, feel that the study of adding ornaments is only useful to those involved in learning older music such as the intricate compositions of J. S. Bach (1685–1750). This is not entirely true. Today's popular music, especially jazz for example, uses improvising to add colourful and creative embellishment. Improvising involves creating music while performing rather than playing a composition that is already completely written down.

One period of music, known as Baroque, dating roughly from 1600 to 1750, does stand apart as a time when ornaments were used extensively. Being able to improvise decoration for a piece of music was a skill required by all musicians, especially solo performers. Composers did not always write out the entire music, but used symbols to indicate ornaments. The musicians were expected to know what to add from the symbols. Many composers of that period were virtuoso performers in their own right, so obviously knew how they wanted to ornament their own work without having to write it out in full. There is also a practical reason for the use of ornamentation in Baroque music. Keyboard music was written for instruments such as the harpsichord and clavichord. Both instruments have a rather dry sound and no way of sustaining a held note. Adding embellishment to a note was a way of making it last longer. As time moved on, musical styles changed and composers notated their music differently. Most of the symbols and signs used a few hundred years ago are no longer seen in music. A few are still used, however, and we will look at each of these briefly. A more in-depth study would be necessary for anyone wanting to perform embellishments, as performance practices depend on the actual style of the music.

Ornaments

THE TRILL

There are different ways of indicating a trill. Sometimes tr or ⌁ is used.

A trill involves quickly alternating between a written pitch and the note above it. Think of a bird trilling! The trill may begin on the written note, or on the upper note and alternate downwards to the written note.

Unmeasured trills are to be performed as quickly as possible, obviously depending on the expertise of the performer. Other trills are measured more accurately. Performing a trill correctly largely depends on the style and period of the music.

Unmeasured trill

Measured trill

THE TURN

The turn is an ornament using four or perhaps five notes. There is a principal note which the other notes move or turn around. The sign for a turn is ∾. Sometimes a trill will finish by using a turn.

Symbol for turn

Example of a trill ending with a turn

GRACE NOTES

A grace note is a very small printed note that is not counted in the general rhythm of the music. It is almost crushed into the note following it. However, in older music, such as that of Bach or Mozart, the grace notes were played more evenly.

Examples of grace notes

Insight

Sometimes performers play grace notes when they don't mean to. In piano playing it happens when you think you have landed on the key you were aiming for, but instead the one next to it is also 'crushed' into the sound. Oops!

Grace notes in older music

MORDENT

The mordent consists of a written note quickly alternated with the note below it. The sign for a mordent is ♈.

The inverted mordent, notated as ᠕, involves alternating between the written note and the note immediately above it.

BROKEN CHORDS

A broken chord, also known as an arpeggio, is represented by a wavy vertical line. This indicates that the notes in the chord are to be played separately in succession, not simultaneously. Anyone strumming across the strings of a guitar is playing a broken chord!

Example of broken chord or arpeggio

🎵 Exercise 17.1 (Listening)

Listen to a demonstration of the ornaments you have studied.

Non-harmonic notes

Non-harmonic notes are different from ornaments in that they are actually written into a melody to add interest and feeling, but do not belong to the accompanying chord. These notes may be found in all styles of music. The most commonly used, the passing note, auxiliary or neighbour note, suspension, anticipation and appoggiatura, will be explained and demonstrated.

PASSING NOTES

The passing note is approached by a step and is also followed by a step. It is usually found on a weak beat and is not sounded with a chord. In the first bar of the example, the overall harmony is that of C major. The notes used on each beat are C, E, G. These are the pitches of a C major triad. The F found on the second half of the second beat functions as a passing note to join the E and G in the melody. In the second bar, the overall harmony is F major. The E and D are used as two consecutive passing notes to link the F and C.

Example using passing notes

Insight

Passing notes are used to add movement and interest to a melody line. These notes are not part of the underlying chord accompaniment. If the passing tones were removed, the melody would still work, although it wouldn't be as interesting.

AUXILIARY OR NEIGHBOUR NOTES

An auxiliary or neighbour note is used between two repeated notes in the melody. It is approached and left by movement of a step, either up or down, and may use either a semitone or a tone. The example shows both upper and lower auxiliary or neighbour notes and uses both semitones and tones.

Example using auxiliary or neighbour notes

SUSPENSION

The suspension is a note belonging to one chord that continues to sound through a change to a new harmony. The suspended note then moves down by step to resolve into a note belonging to the new chord. Using a suspension is a good way to create a feeling of tension which is then quickly resolved.

Example using suspensions

ANTICIPATION

An anticipation is the opposite of the suspension. Instead of holding a note over into the new harmony, it anticipates a note from the new harmony before the chord is actually sounded. The anticipation is often found at the end of a piece.

Example showing anticipation

APPOGGIATURA

The appoggiatura is an accented non-harmonic note. This means that the dissonance is sounded on a strong beat. The appoggiatura is approached by a skip in the melody and resolved by step in the opposite direction of the skip. The word is Italian, roughly meaning to lean. The non-harmonic note does not belong to the harmony and is leaning into the chord, creating a dissonance which must be resolved.

Example of the appoggiatura

F

 Exercise 17.2 (Listening)

Listen to the examples of the different non-harmonic notes.

GOALS

1 *Understand the difference between ornaments and non-harmonic notes.*
2 *Know the basic notation for different ornaments.*
3 *Be able to recognize ornaments as they are played.*
4 *Know the basic notation of non-harmonic notes.*
5 *Be able to recognize non-harmonic notes when they are played.*

TEST YOURSELF

1 Name the period of music, dating between 1600 and 1750, where ornamentation was used extensively.

2 Describe a trill.

3 This ornament starts on the note above the written note, then moves to the written note itself, then to the note below. What is it called?

4 Name a very small note, printed before the main note, and not counted in the general rhythm of the music.

5 Give another name for a broken chord.

6 Do non-harmonic notes belong to the accompanying chord?

7 How is a passing note approached and followed?

8 Must an auxiliary or neighbour note be a semitone (half tone)?

9 Which non-harmonic note is good for creating a feeling of tension?

10 Where, in a piece of music, might an anticipation be found?

18

Music theory in the 20th century

Classical music of the 20th century has developed in a variety of ways. The theory has incorporated a wide range of ideas from the past and combined them in new, innovative ways. There is more use of dissonance, new scales have been devised and rhythms are more irregular. This chapter briefly explores some of the ways in which music theory has changed in more recent years.

Chords

During the past century, there has been much experimentation in building chords in new ways. Triads with added notes of the ninth, 11th and 13th are found much more often. This causes the key or tonal centre to become vague. Chords are also built by using the interval of a fourth, not the third, and the augmented fourth (tritone) is left unresolved. This adds more dissonance and blurring of the tonal centre. Other chords are also constructed of dissonant seconds, many written as clusters with all of the notes of a scale clustered together.

Insight

Many people are put off listening to contemporary music due to the often dissonant and strange sound. I have heard such comments as, 'where is the melody?' or 'it doesn't sound like music!' It is important to approach new music with an open mind. It really can't be compared to older music because of the new and different ways it is constructed.

Exercise 18.1 (Listening)

Study the examples of chords constructed in various ways. Listen to a demonstration on the CD.

a) Chords constructed using seconds

b) Chords constructed using fourths

c) Clusters

Insight

If you want to remind yourself of what a chord constructed using seconds or a chord cluster sounds like, think of a kitten walking up and down a piano keyboard. It's a very similar sound!

Atonality

Following World War I there was a period of intense experimentation with music theory. Composers such as Arnold Schoenberg worked at getting rid of traditional harmony, especially the tonal centre, by using a 12-note row. Each composition is based on a series or row made of all 12 chromatic notes arranged in a specific order by the composer. The order of the row stays the same throughout the work, but may be varied by transposing it by octaves, changing the rhythm or using the row backwards. Because there is no tonal centre or key, each of the 12 chromatic notes being equal in status, this type of music is referred to as atonal.

Example of a 12-note row

Exercise 18.2 (Listening)

Listen to a demonstration of the 12-note row.

Other scales

Besides the use of the 12-note row, composers also devised their own scales called synthetic scales. Two different scales may be found placed against one another in a sort of counterpoint. This creates two different tonal centres and is called polytonal music. Placing two different modes such as major or minor together creates polymodal music.

Examples of polytonal and polymodal music

Exercise 18.3 (Listening)

Listen to a demonstration of polytonal and polymodal music.

The whole tone scale is built completely of whole tones and has only seven notes in the octave. For example, the notes in the C octave are C, D, E, F♯, G♯, A♯ and C. This scale does not include the interval of the perfect fourth or perfect fifth and has no leading note. Again, there is a loss of tonal feeling since all the notes in the scale are equal. The pentatonic scale has only five notes and is often found in the music of China and Africa. Different pentatonic scales have been used in 20th-century music, but the most common are C, D, E, G, A and C, D♭, E♭, G, A. The black keys of the piano keyboard form a pentatonic scale. Note that any pitch can be the starting point for these different scales, just as in major and minor scales.

Examples of whole tone and pentatonic scales

Exercise 18.4 (Written)

Construct a whole tone scale beginning on the following notes:

a)

b)

⊘ Exercise 18.5 (Listening)

Listen to a demonstration of whole tone and pentatonic scales.

> **Insight**
> After listening to the examples of the whole tone and
> pentatonic scales, try humming or singing them. First, work
> on the whole tone scale until you are able to sing it starting
> on various pitches. When that becomes easy, work on
> the pentatonic scale the same way. This practice will help
> establish the sounds of these two different scales.

Neoclassical ideas

Following the period of experimentation at the start of the
20th century, the 1920s saw a return to an interest in past styles
and forms in music. Once again counterpoint was used in new
compositions. These works, however, also incorporated some of the
new innovations. The individual melody lines were written without
regard for a single tonal centre. Elements from folk music were fused
with more complex music. This is especially true in the music of the
Hungarian composer Béla Bartók. The influence of jazz, which was
developing in the USA, can also be seen in works of this period.

> **Insight**
> Since the CD doesn't contain any examples of folk elements
> combined with complex music, see if you can find some
> Hungarian folk songs by Béla Bartók. For added jazz
> elements, try listening to the music of George Gershwin.

Other innovations

During the second half of the 20th century, there were again
more attempts in experimenting with sounds. One example is the

'prepared' piano used by the composer John Cage. He artificially altered the sound of a piano by inserting objects such as felt, paper, rubber wedges or metal into the strings. In France, a practice known as *musique concrète* used recordings of noises and everyday sounds as the basic material, not musical notes. These practices, however, were not mainstream.

Insight

If possible, I would recommend listening to a piece for prepared piano. It can be very rhythmic sounding. You may not like what you hear, but at least you've heard it! And the same goes for *musique concrète*!

The future

It is unclear what directions music theory will follow in the 21st century. All indications show that there will not only be further experimentation, but also interesting new uses of established practices. One composer, Mark-Anthony Turnage, combines contemporary classical music with modern jazz. There is no doubt that the possibilities for new musical creativity in the future are endless!

GOALS

1 *Know some of the new ways chords were constructed in the 20th century.*
2 *Understand how a 12-note row is constructed.*
3 *Define 'polytonal' and 'polymodal'.*
4 *Be able to construct a whole tone scale, starting on different pitches.*

Answers

EXERCISE 18.4

a)

b)

TEST YOURSELF

1 What happens to the tonal centre if lots of added note chords are used?

2 Describe a chord cluster.

3 Are all of the notes in a 12-note row equal in status?

4 Music containing the C major scale written against the C minor scale is called what?

5 The groups of three and two black keys on the piano keyboard form which type of scale?

6 Which two intervals are missing in a whole tone scale?

7 What else is missing from the whole tone scale?

8 Name two elements that were fused with complex music of the 1920s.

9 What did John Cage do to the piano?

10 Recordings of noises and everyday sounds used as basic material for compositions are called what?

Answers to 'Test yourself' questions

Chapter 1

1 *Anything associated with the duration of a sound.*
2 *As notes.*
3 *Its shape.*
4 *A vertical line that divides music into equal segments.*
5 *The top number tells how many beats per bar. The bottom tells the type of note that gets the basic beat.*
6 *Quarter note.*
7 *The relationships of the note values are visually represented, making reading the music easier.*
8 *Two beats.*
9 *A rest.*
10 *The speed at which music is played.*

Chapter 2

1 *The lowness or highness of a sound.*
2 *Seven.*
3 *Higher.*
4 *In patterns of white and black keys.*
5 *Five lines and four spaces between the lines.*
6 *Treble and bass.*
7 *Middle C.*
8 *C D E F G.*
9 *C B A G F.*
10 *When movement is to the note directly above or below the previous one.*

Chapter 3

1 *Melody.*
2 *An organized series of different pitches.*
3 *Repetition.*
4 *Use exact repetition.*
5 *Repetition of second bar rhythm; second bar rhythm used in reverse; or make the fourth bar identical to the second bar.*
6 *The basic pulse.*
7 *By a curved line.*
8 *The sense of direction in a melody.*
9 *The mood of the music.*
10 *Starting low and ending high; or starting low, moving higher, ending low.*

Chapter 4

1 *An octave.*
2 *Bottom line and fourth space.*
3 *Top line and first space.*
4 *Upwards.*
5 *Downwards.*
6 *The stem may go in either direction to fit into the context.*
7 *Short, added lines drawn above or below the staff.*
8 *It shows that a note will sound either an octave higher or an octave lower than written.*
9 *Middle line.*
10 *Second line from the top.*

Chapter 5

1 *Waltz time.*
2 *Three.*
3 *A dot.*

4 *A note carried over into the following bar by a curved line.*
5 *It only lasts half of one count.*
6 *A semiquaver or sixteenth note only lasts half as long as a quaver or eighth note.*
7 *A beat that is divided into three equal parts.*
8 *A quaver or eight note.*
9 *An incomplete bar.*
10 *The displacement of the expected accent.*

Chapter 6

1 *Sharp.*
2 *Before the note and on the same line or space.*
3 *Accidentals.*
4 *One bar.*
5 *After the letter-name.*
6 *A bar-line.*
7 *No. A higher pitched F will also need an added sharp.*
8 *A double sharp.*
9 *A double flat.*
10 *G.*

Chapter 7

1 *A semitone or half tone.*
2 *Two.*
3 *B.*
4 *Perfect.*
5 *Nine.*
6 *Diminished.*
7 *It also becomes diminished.*
8 *Three.*
9 *By moving the lower note an octave higher or the higher note an octave lower.*
10 *Ninth, tenth, 11th, 12th or 13th.*

Chapter 8

1 *Intervals linked together to form a melody.*
2 *Perfect fourth.*
3 *Perfect fifth.*
4 *Performing music at sight.*
5 *By studying the intervals and the direction they move.*
6 *Moving all of the pitches in a piece of music the same distance up or down.*
7 *It would sound wrong when the transposed melody is played.*
8 *G above that C.*
9 *C below that D.*
10 *Add a little each time.*

Chapter 9

1 *An alphabetical succession of notes, starting on a particular pitch.*
2 *The arrangement of the pitches.*
3 *Modes.*
4 *T T S T T T S*
5 *Degrees.*
6 *F and C sharps.*
7 *F, C and G sharps.*
8 *F, C, G and D sharps.*
9 *No. Only use one or the other, not both.*
10 *B, E and A flats.*

Chapter 10

1 *A to A.*
2 *The sixth and seventh degrees are raised one semitone or half tone when ascending, but lowered again when descending.*

3 *The seventh degree is raised one semitone or half tone both ascending and descending.*

4 *T S T T S T T.*

5 *E flat raised to E natural.*

6 *Three flats.*

7 *Both A flat and B flat are raised one semitone or half tone ascending, but lowered descending.*

8 *No, they are relative key signatures.*

9 *They are relative key signatures.*

10 *The third and seventh degrees are lowered.*

Chapter 11

1 *Compound.*

2 *Two.*

3 *Six beats, the quaver or eighth note gets the beat.*

4 *Quaver or eighth note.*

5 *Still the quaver or eighth note.*

6 $\frac{2}{4}$.

7 $\frac{4}{4}$.

8 *No, it is a simple duple metre.*

9 *On the first and third or first and fourth beats.*

10 *On the first and fourth or first and fifth beats.*

Chapter 12

1 *Three or more notes sounded together.*

2 *A chord consisting of three notes.*

3 *Major and minor.*

4 *Root position.*

5 *The interval between the root and third is a minor third, not a major third.*

6 *An inversion.*

7 *No, just the order.*

8 *Augmented.*

9 *A letter-name representing a chord, usually written above the melody line.*

10 *A basic triad with extra notes added to give colour and interest.*

Chapter 13

1 *Harmonic*

2 *I, IV and V.*

3 *Plagal cadence.*

4 *The root note.*

5 *To the tonic note.*

6 $\frac{6}{3}$.

7 *No, it is counterpoint or polyphonic writing.*

8 *A short melodic figure used in counterpoint.*

9 *A transition chord common to both the new and original keys.*

10 *Yes.*

Chapter 14

1 *Make a chord chart showing the triads of each scale degree.*

2 *I, IV and V.*

3 *Minor.*

4 *Only when necessary, once or twice per bar.*

5 *The C major chord establishes the key feeling.*

6 *No. Ending on the C major chord is necessary for the key feeling.*

7 *To move it to a more comfortable key for singing or playing.*

8 *Yes, or it will sound wrong.*

9 *Melody is written in treble clef for the right hand. Chord accompaniment is written in the bass clef for left hand.*

10 *Inversions make moving between chords easier.*

Chapter 15

1 *Form.*
2 *Two vertical lines with two dots placed to the left.*
3 *No. Skip over the first time bar and only play the second time bar.*
4 *Return to the beginning of the work and play until reaching the word 'fine.'*
5 *A B.*
6 *A B A C A D A E A.*
7 *Movements.*
8 *Exposition, development, recapitulation.*
9 *Fast.*
10 *The lyrics.*

Chapter 16

1 *Different instruments have an individual tone colour or timbre.*
2 *Orchestration.*
3 *No.*
4 *No, only the ones actually playing on a particular page.*
5 *The left hand.*
6 *Tempo, meaning slow.*
7 *An instrument that clicks at a set rate. Useful for learning to play to a strict beat.*
8 *Go back to the original speed.*
9 *Levels of loudness and softness in music.*
10 *The way an individual note is performed.*

Chapter 17

1 *Baroque*
2 *An ornament alternating between a written pitch and the note above it.*

3 *A turn.*
4 *A grace note.*
5 *Arpeggio.*
6 *No.*
7 *By step.*
8 *No. Whole tones may be used.*
9 *Suspension.*
10 *At the end.*

Chapter 18

1 *It becomes vague.*
2 *A chord constructed of dissonant seconds, with all of the notes of the scale clustered together.*
3 *Yes.*
4 *Polymodal.*
5 *Pentatonic scale.*
6 *The perfect fourth and the perfect fifth.*
7 *The leading note.*
8 *Folk music and jazz.*
9 *Prepared it, artificially altering the sound.*
10 *Musique concrète.*

Taking it further

Listed below are suggestions for further study of music theory and related musical activities:

The Associated Board of the Royal Schools of Music
14 Bedford Square
London WC1B 3JG
United Kingdom
www.abrsm.org/publishing

The Associated Board provides graded music for a wide variety of instruments and voice. It also has published a music theory textbook, *The AB Guide to Music Theory*, and graded music theory workbooks. The emphasis is mainly classical, although some jazz has recently been introduced.

For students interested in applying music theory to piano or electronic keyboard, *The Complete Piano Player* and *The Complete Keyboard Player* are useful books. These are written by Kenneth Baker and published by Wise Publications.

Advice on finding a private music teacher:

- *Recommendation by word of mouth.*
- *Some public libraries keep lists of local teachers.*
- *Check adverts in local newspapers.*
- *Contact local colleges or universities. Many advanced music students offer individual lessons.*

Opportunities for group learning:

- *Many adult education centres and local colleges offer various day or evening classes in music.*

► *Local groups such as choirs or brass bands often provide free instruction in reading and performing music.*

The British and International Music Yearbook, published by Rhinegold, is an extensive directory containing information on education, music venues and music book publishers.

Rhinegold Publishing Ltd.
241 Shaftesbury Avenue
London WC2H 8EH
www.rhinegold.co.uk

There are many websites which sell music books and sheet music of all types. A few are listed below:

www.musicexchange.com
www.sheetmusicdirect.com
www.musicroom.com
www.sheetmusicplus.com
www.lookmusic.com

Glossary

Musical terms used in this book

accent special stress or emphasis given to a note

accidental symbol written as needed before a pitch to raise or lower it

accompaniment musical background added to the main melody

alto second highest voice in four-part chorale writing; a low female voice

alto clef clef using the third line of a staff as middle C; mainly used for notating music for viola

arrangement music adapted for performance in a different way from how it was originally written

augment make larger; applies to intervals and chords

bar (measure) space between two bar-lines

bar-line vertical line dividing written music into bars, each containing the number of beats shown by the time signature

bass lowest male voice in four-part chorale writing

bass clef see **F clef**

beam a line used to group notes together, in place of their individual tails

beat underlying pulse of each bar which is counted

brace bracket joining two or more staves together

breve note held twice as long as a semibreve (not often used in modern notation)

C clef clef used to locate middle C on either the third or fourth line of a staff

cadence chord progression found at the end of a phrase, section or entire work

chord three or more pitches played or sung together

chord symbol letter-name representing a chord, written above a melody line to show the chord accompaniment

clef sign placed at the beginning of a work to indicate a certain pitch

coda extra bars added to the end of a composition

common time ⁴₄ time, sometimes abbreviated as C instead of the numbers

compound interval interval larger than an octave

compound time time signature where each beat of the bar is divided into three (♩♩♩)

counterpoint melodies written against one another; linear music

crotchet (quarter note) note receiving one-quarter the value of a semibreve

degrees individual notes of a scale

diminish make smaller; applies to intervals and chords

dotted note note receiving half the value again of its original length

double bar-lines vertical lines marking the end of a work or section of a large composition

double flat sign which lowers an already flattened note

doubled sharp sign which raises an already sharpened note

duet music for two performers

dynamics varying loudness and softness in music

eighth note see **quaver**

F clef clef marking the fourth line as the F below middle C; also known as bass clef

fine end of a work, the finish

flat sign which lowers the pitch of a note by one semitone

G clef clef marking the second line as G above middle C; also known as treble clef

grace note ornamental note of short duration

half note see **minim**

half tone see **semitone**

harmony study of combinations of pitches, mainly chords

interval distance or space between two pitches

inversion change in the order of notes in a chord

key tonal centre based on a scale; also, a lever depressed on a
    keyboard

keynote first note of a scale

key signature sharps or flats shown on the staff at the
    beginning of a line of music

leger (ledger) line short line added above or below the staff
    as needed

measure see **bar**

melody organized series of pitches

metre basic scheme of beats; same as time signature

metronome machine which beats time at a set pulse

middle C first leger line both below the treble staff and
    above the bass staff; also, the C nearest the middle of
    the keyboard

minim (half note) note receiving half the value of a semibreve

natural sign cancels a sharp or flat

notation writing music down

note a musical sound with a definite pitch (Brit.); symbol used
    to show the length and pitch of a musical sound

octave interval consisting of the eight notes of any scale,
    covering the distance between one note and the next one
    higher or lower with the same letter-name

ornament embellishment added to music, usually to the melody line

phrase section of music, similar to a sentence in language

pitch highness or lowness of a musical sound

quarter note see **crotchet**

quaver (eighth note) note receiving half the value of a crotchet

repeat sign sign consisting of vertical double lines and matching dots showing that the music in between is to be repeated

rest symbol indicating a period of silence

rhythm notes of various duration organized into patterns to fit a time signature

scale series of alphabetically arranged pitches

score written music showing all the parts for various instruments and voices on one page

semibreve (whole note) note with the longest duration found in most modern music notation

semiquaver (sixteenth note) note receiving half the value of a quaver

semitone (half tone) smallest interval in music notation

sharp sign raising a pitch one semitone

simple time time signature where each beat of the bar is divided by 2 (e.g. $\frac{2}{4}$)

sixteenth note see **semiquaver**

slur curved line drawn above or below the heads of two or more consecutive notes to show they should be played smoothly

solo (for) one performer only

soprano highest female voice in four-part vocal writing

staccato detached, short

staff (stave) five lines and four spaces on which music is notated

syncopation displaced accents put on normally weak beats

tempo speed of a piece of music

tenor highest male voice in four-part vocal writing

tenor clef C clef placing middle C on the fourth line of the staff

tie curved line joining two notes of the same pitch, adding length to the duration of the original note

time signature two numbers or a sign placed at the beginning of music, the top number showing the number of beats in each bar, the bottom number giving the value of the note receiving one beat

tone (whole tone) interval made of two semitones; also a musical sound with a definite pitch (US)

tonic first degree of a scale

transposing to write or perform music in a different key or octave from that in which it was originally written

treble clef see **G clef**

triad chord containing three notes

trill ornament performed by quick alternation between the given note and the note either above or below it

triplet group of notes which takes the place of two of the same kind (e.g. two quavers); notated by a 3 and a bracket

tritone dissonant interval of the augmented fourth/diminished fifth

unison two notes having the same pitch

waltz dance written in $\frac{3}{4}$ time

whole note see **semibreve**

Italian terms commonly used in music

a cappella unaccompanied voices

accelerando (accel.) gradually becoming faster

adagio leisurely, slow tempo

agitato excited, agitated

allegretto lively tempo, not as fast as allegro

allegro cheerful, quick tempo

andante moderate, walking speed

andantino slightly faster than andante

animato animated, with spirit

assai very

a tempo return to the original speed

brio brilliance, spirit

cantabile in a singing style

con with

crescendo (cresc.) gradually becoming louder

decrescendo gradually becoming softer

diminuendo (dim.) gradually becoming softer

dolce sweetly

espressivo with expression

forte (f) loud

forte piano (fp) loud, then suddenly soft

fortissimo (ff) very loud

giocoso playfully

grave slow, solemn

grazioso gracefully

larghetto slow but not as slow as largo

largo slow, stately tempo, slower than **lento**

legato smooth and connected manner of playing or singing

lento slow but not as slow as **largo**

maestoso majestically

marcato marked, accented

meno less

mezzo forte (mf) medium loud

mezzo piano (mp) medium soft

moderato at a moderate speed

molto very

moto motion

non not

pesante heavy

pianissimo (pp) very soft

piano (p) soft

più more

poco little

prestissimo as quickly as possible

presto very fast

prima, primo first

quasi similar to

rallentando (rall.) gradually becoming slower

ritardando growing slower

ritenuto (rit.) growing slower

rubato with freedom in the rhythm

scherzando playfully

semplice simply

sempre always

senza without

sforzando (sfz) suddenly loud

simile the same

sostenuto sustained

subito suddenly

tranquillo quiet

vivace quick, lively tempo

vivo lively

Note that some of the words, such as **con** (with) or **senza** (without), are combined to give instructions to the performer.

Note values

semibreve (whole note)	
minim (half note)	
crotchet (quarter note)	
quaver (eighth note)	
semiquaver (sixteenth note)	
demi-semiquaver (thirty-second note)	

Rests

	semibreve (whole note)
	minim (half note)
	crotchet (quarter note)
	quaver (eighth note)
	semiquaver (sixteenth note)
	demi-semiquaver (thirty-second note)

Table of key signatures

Major

Minor

Notes on the staff

Index

Image credits

Front cover: © Ilovephoto Design/Photodisc/Getty Images

Back cover: © Jakub Semeniuk/iStockphoto.com, © Royalty-Free/Corbis, © agencyby/iStockphoto.com, © Andy Cook/iStockphoto.com, © Christopher Ewing/iStockphoto.com, © zebicho – Fotolia.com, © Geoffrey Holman/iStockphoto.com, © Photodisc/Getty Images, © James C. Pruitt/iStockphoto.com, © Mohamed Saber – Fotolia.com